Praise for
The Learning Game

"Is it possible that we all hope for the same things for our children? We want them to be kind, capable, collaborative, and curious. What do schools want for the kids they serve? Do they focus on adherence to a system of rules, standards, and protocols incompatible with reality, or do they spend time on what really matters? *The Learning Game* reminds us what is lost when we focus on winning the game of school. We know that our children shouldn't spend a thousand hours each year sitting in rows and laboring through worksheets to "earn" a grade. Ana Lorena provides an incisive critique of our current approach to education and outlines a compelling vision of what learning ought to be: collaborative, relevant, challenging, and fun."

— Joshua Dahn, Co-Founder, Synthesis and Ad Astra

"Ana Lorena has delivered an essential read—a piercing critique of our education system and a practical plan for reform. This book is a call to action for parents, educators, and policy makers to overturn the status quo, reimagine learning, and do right by our kids."

— Daniel H. Pink, #1 *New York Times* Bestselling Author, *Drive*, *When*, and *A Whole New Mind*

"This is a must-read for every parent, every taxpayer and anyone who cares about how our future will unfold. Ana Lorena's urgent and insightful common sense is precisely what we need to move forward."

— Seth Godin, Author, *The Song of Significance*

"Ana Lorena's new book *The Learning Game* should be required reading for all educators trying to reimagine how we can overhaul the antiquated methods we use in teaching our children. Kids are natural learners—but to help them supercharge it, we need to make it exciting, fun, and more about *how* to think rather than *what* to think. What if we synthesize kids' natural curiosity, ability to question, and desire to play and have fun with a new curriculum and way of teaching? In that case, I think the results will astound us. I highly recommend this book."

— Jim O'Shaughnessy, Founder & CEO, O'Shaughnessy Ventures LLC

"Ana Lorena presents a new model of education that transforms the learning process into a truly engaging and fulfilling experience. Get ready to revolutionize the way you approach education and inspire a lifelong love of learning in kids."

— Amjad Masad, Founder and CEO, Replit

"As a new father, I find myself spending a lot of time thinking about what my son's education will look like and how we can do things differently to create a better experience for him than I ever had. *The Learning Game* is a brilliant look into the future of education innovation. With people like Ana Lorena leading the way, I am hopeful that the future will look much better than the past!"

— Sahil Bloom, Writer and Investor

"Throughout my career working with elite professional athletes and coaches, one thing is evident—the ability to learn is a competitive advantage. If you are a parent, teacher, or coach and are serious about setting your child up for future success, *The Learning Game* is a must-read. Ana Lorena provides evidence-based mental models and tools in a practical, easy-to-read manner that will help you create an environment to unlock your child's creativity, critical thinking, and intellectual independence. Ana Lorena is a master teacher; her ability to simplify complex concepts makes it easy for the reader to understand and apply these principles with your child immediately."

— Justin Su'a, Head of Mental Performance, Tampa Bay Rays

The
Learning
Game

Every owner of a physical copy of this edition of

The
Learning
Game

can download the eBook for free direct from us at
Harriman House, in a DRM-free format that can be read
on any eReader, tablet or smartphone.

Simply head to:

ebooks.harriman-house.com/learninggame

to get your copy now.

The
Learning
Game

Teaching Kids to Think
for Themselves, Embrace
Challenge, and Love Learning

Ana Lorena Fábrega

Harriman
House

HARRIMAN HOUSE LTD
3 Viceroy Court
Bedford Road
Petersfield
Hampshire
GU32 3LJ
GREAT BRITAIN
Tel: +44 (0)1730 233870

Email: enquiries@harriman-house.com
Website: harriman.house

First published in 2023.
Copyright © Ana Lorena Fábrega

The right of Ana Lorena Fábrega to be identified as the Author has been asserted in accordance with the Copyright, Design and Patents Act 1988.

Hardback ISBN: 978-1-80409-009-1
Paperback ISBN: 978-1-80409-051-0
eBook ISBN: 978-1-80409-010-7

British Library Cataloguing in Publication Data
A CIP catalogue record for this book can be obtained from the British Library.

To my son, Fer.
Stay curious ♥

Contents

Foreword
by David Perell

I KNEW ANA was destined for greatness from the moment I met her. Maybe it was her fire for teaching. Maybe it was the intensity she brought to her own learning. Or maybe, I was just amazed with the clarity of her vision for education.

When I met her, she hadn't written much of anything. She was a frustrated schoolteacher who'd recently retired from classroom teaching because the system didn't work for her or her students.

But we've shared a vision since the day we met. Like Ana, I've devoted my professional life to improving the way we learn. Both of us are fed up with how the system is explicitly designed to manufacture a docile and obedient population. We believe that schools should graduate lifelong learners, who brim with curiosity instead. Too many kids love learning, but hate school. It's time to change that.

When I met Ana, she was one of my students. My course, Write of Passage, inspired her to write and publish consistently for the first time. Watching her tweets go viral and the size of her audience explode showed me how desperately people wanted to shake up the school system and build something new. Following

Ana is a peek into the future of education. In her writings, she lays out the map that our children and grandchildren will follow.

Ana stands out for her digitally native approach. Ana's writing is fresh because she's synthesized a new set of ideas. In addition to pulling from the canon of educational theory, she's incorporated ideas from the worlds of gaming, investing, and entrepreneurship. She's broken free from the system. Instead of rejecting technology, she embraces it. Instead of looking down on kids, she respects them. She's charted her own path with such charisma that she's attracted a legion of parents and teachers from around the world.

Her ideas are enhanced by her time in the classroom. In addition to almost a decade of in-person teaching experience, she attended ten schools in seven different countries as a kid. That diversity of experience enables her originality of thought.

As a writer, Ana is different from her peers too. So much of what I read about education is dry and over-intellectualized, but Ana's writing is unique. It's bubbly, imaginative, and informed by decades of experience.

Inside the classroom, two stories reveal Ana's impact. Her students adore her so much that 19 of them made a surprise visit to her wedding. When Ana and I ran an educational summer camp for kids, a parent emailed us to say that the weight of her daughter's depression had lifted off her shoulders because she was so inspired by Ana's teaching.

Then there's Ana's productive rebellion. While other teachers crammed for standardized test preparation, Ana had the courage to stand up against the system and deliver her own curriculum (and yet, her class placed first in math and reading on the MAPS test).

The world needs this book. Our schools are relics of the industrial age. They prize obedience over curiosity. In the name of "learning," they've become anti-curiosity machines. Despite all the advancements in technology and learning science, our schools basically look the same today as they did 100 years ago. Too many students are uninspired, unmotivated, and unengaged.

In *The Learning Game*, Ana presents some unconventional solutions to the troubles of education. In a world of awards for high performance, Ana said no to rewards. While kids in other classrooms were narrowly restricted to the syllabus, Ana gave her students free rein to follow their curiosity with projects of their own. She also taught through captivating stories instead of tedious facts, figures, and formulas.

This book comes at an inflection point for learning. The internet and high-speed computing are among the best things to ever happen to education.

As Ana writes, the internet makes it uniquely possible for kids to teach themselves. It's time to move beyond our one-size-fits-all system. In our world of information abundance, curiosity has become the rate limiter on learning. We must teach kids to teach themselves.

This book is written for schools that want to change their ways, students who want to love learning, and parents who are frustrated with the options for their children. It's a peek into what education could be, if only we had the gumption to build a system for the way the world is, not how it used to be.

David Perell
September, 2023

I Was a Teacher,
I Loved It, I Quit

GROWING UP, I attended ten schools in seven countries: Panama, Colombia, Venezuela, India, Mexico, Brazil, and the United States.

I was constantly surrounded by new languages, cultures, and social norms. Not to mention each school was different: international, local, public, private, secular, religious...

We moved countries frequently, sometimes in the middle of the school year. On occasion, I had to repeat grades because I got there at an awkward time, or because I didn't know the language yet.

It was A LOT to take in as a kid. I was always the new girl.

Looking back, I was fortunate to adapt pretty well despite all the changes.

My parents say it's because I was a very social and personable kid. And yes, that helped me make friends and made things easier. But I'd argue that my personality is not how I kept up with new academic environments and expectations.

I adapted because I figured out how to play the *game of school*.

In the game of school, you succeed by pleasing your teachers, getting good grades, and advancing to the next grade. You win if you follow the rules of order, obedience, and compliance.

Sit up. Be quiet. Pretend to pay attention. Raise your hand to speak. Do as you are told. Don't question things. Follow a bell schedule. Fill out worksheets. I became a master at this.

But the game of school didn't help me learn. In fact, I quickly realized school was more of an *imitation* of learning.

For me, real learning happened when I was exploring my curiosities and unleashing my creativity. This happened outside of the classroom: when I would come up with skits and dance choreographies, create my own board games, design wedding dresses for my dolls, turn my playroom into a museum, build forts, make mud pies, find geometric patterns in nature walks, solve my own mysteries, and then write about all of it in my diary.

I adapted because I figured out how to play the game of school.

I came to see these activities as my learning game.

The game of school was what I did in the classroom. And the learning game—where I was really learning—was what I did outside the classroom.

Succeeding at the game of school, I figured, would grant me approval to do all the things I really wanted to do in my own time.

I played the game over and over again until I graduated high school. I was good at it, but I didn't like it.

What I did enjoy was learning itself. I was profusely curious and could talk for hours about my musings. Engaging in my own projects energized me, and I had a natural way of explaining things and capturing people's attention.

And so upon leaving high school, I decided to become an educator to share my passion for learning with others.

I got degrees in Childhood Education, Special Education, and Psychology, while I student-taught in five different schools in New York City. I got to see hundreds of kids from all ages and backgrounds in the classroom. And that's when it dawned on me.

No matter the school, the students were told: Sit up. Be quiet. Pay attention. Raise your hand to speak. Do as you are told. Don't question why.

These students were also playing the game of school. I recognized the game; I was an expert in it myself!

But it had never occurred to me that the game was universal.

This opened my eyes to where education is stuck. Kids are stuck in the game of school, imitating their teachers instead of thinking for themselves, losing points for mistakes instead of learning from them, coloring inside the lines instead of thinking outside the box, and waiting for instructions instead of figuring things out.

I realized if we want kids to really learn, they can't be stuck in the game of school.

When I got my own classroom, I tried to do things differently. And, to a certain extent, I did.

I wanted to create a student-centered environment that made it easy to want to come to school every day. I pushed my students to seek their own interests and explore their passions, even when this meant deviating from school parameters. I tried to be flexible, providing choices so that my students felt empowered to take ownership over their learning. I encouraged them to question everything—"Says who?" "What's the counter argument?" "What side of the story is not being told?"

> Kids are stuck in the game of school, imitating their teachers instead of thinking for themselves.

> **Young children are curious and have a built-in desire to learn. As they get older and enter school, learning becomes forced. No wonder they lose interest.**

"Can someone try to prove this wrong?"—and figure things out for themselves.

Most importantly, I tried to instill in my students a love for learning. I knew that if I succeeded, their academic and life success would follow. My hope was that my students would continue to carry a passion for learning through the rest of their lives.

But to my surprise, as students moved on to the next grade, they became less interested and forgot the joy of learning. Many stopped taking risks and asking questions, and others began to dread things they used to love, like reading and writing.

They stopped playing the game of learning and were dragged back into the game of school.

It seemed like a common trend, even for students who moved on to good teachers in middle and high school.

Why had my students lost their interest in learning?

Young children are curious and have a built-in desire to learn. As they get older and enter school, learning becomes forced. Students have no choice in the subjects, the pace, or the way lessons are presented. They enter a system that leaves little room for choice and exploration, even when individual teachers try to create it. No wonder they lose interest and defer to the game of school.

I started questioning our education system and my role in it.

How can teachers cultivate in students a love for learning that lasts forever, when they are forced to teach a one-size-fits-all curriculum that rewards grades and standards over creativity and choice?

After years of teaching, I made the hard decision to leave the school system. There had to be a better way...

I started asking a new set of questions:

- How can we transform the game of school into the game of learning?
- How do we make learning sustainable through childhood and into adulthood?
- How can we go back to the root of what makes kids excited to learn?
- How can we arm kids with the tools they need to succeed in the game of learning—and the game of life?

The Learning Game is my attempt to answer these questions. It's a collection of my work, lessons, and findings since I quit teaching. It's about how to challenge things we've all taken for granted, from the roots of our education system to the modern school curriculum.

But it's not just a book about school. First and foremost, it's a book about *kids*.

Kids are the inventors and explorers of the future. It is our responsibility to question again and again whether their learning circumstances are enabling them to reach their full potential. If we don't course-correct their learning trajectory, who will?

Now, my goal is not to convince you to take your kids out of school tomorrow (although you may decide to do that). Rather, it's to help you realize why traditional schooling no longer meets the needs of our kids today.

We owe it to kids to help them leave behind the game of school. They deserve to play a better, more important game—one that is relevant to them and our world of constant change. One that you and they design together. And that is what this book is about.

You may read this book however you like. It's short enough for power readers to finish in one sitting, but you could also read one

~~School~~

1

Seven Dangerous Lessons Taught in Schools

J OHN TAYLOR GATTO was a celebrated educator in the New York City school system, honored multiple times as Teacher of the Year.

When he won the award for the third time in a row in 1991, he wrote an article for *The Wall Street Journal*. You might expect him to have a long list of thank yous for the industry, or talk about the importance of public education. Instead, he opened the article this way:

> I've taught public school for 26 years but I just can't do it anymore. For years I asked the local school board and superintendent to let me teach a curriculum that doesn't hurt kids, but they had other fish to fry. So I'm going to quit.[1]

The announcement shook many. The most influential educator in New York City was not only quitting the system, but also denouncing it?

Gatto didn't stop there—a few months later he published a book. In *Dumbing Us Down: The Hidden Curriculum of Compulsory Schooling*,[2] Gatto describes the problem with constraining teachers on what to teach.

Gatto was an exceptional educator who cared deeply for his students and their preparation. And yet, he was the first to call out how our education system hurts kids more than it helps them.

Who better than Gatto to help us understand how traditional teaching methods have gone in the wrong direction?

In *Dumbing Us Down,* Gatto outlines seven "dangerous" lessons that the system forces educators to teach students. In this chapter, we'll use these lessons to diagnose the current state of the education system. We'll also lay out a few ideas on how we need to reinvent our methods of teaching others—and ourselves.

Let's start unpacking each of these lessons.

Lesson 1: Confusion

The sequence of school curricula forces kids to learn each subject in isolation. Gatto said:

> Everything I teach is out of context. I teach the un-relating of everything. I teach disconnections. I teach too much: the orbiting of planets, the law of large numbers, slavery, adjectives, architectural drawing, dance, gymnasium, choral singing, assemblies, surprise guests, fire drills, computer languages, parents' nights, staff-development days, pull-out programs, guidance with strangers my students may never see again, standardized tests, age-segregation unlike anything seen in the outside world… What do any of these things have to do with each other?[3]

School curricula don't help kids build a coherent picture of how the real world works. Students learn trigonometry but rarely get a chance to build anything. They miss the chance to see how the *hypotenuse* can be applied in practice, like when designing a house. No wonder kids become confused about how things fit together!

What if instead of teaching lots of things in isolation, we taught them in context? Kids internalize concepts best when using them to build relevant projects or solve real problems.

Tools acquired *in context* are far more useful in the real world.

We use code when we want to build a website. We use math when we want to make a budget. We brush up on English when we want to write about a topic we love. Without this focus and context, learning becomes boring and pointless.

LEARN THEORY...   **...IN CONTEXT**

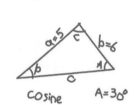

Lesson 2: Class Position

Schools obsess over putting every kid in their proper place. Gatto wrote:

> I teach that students must stay in the class where they belong. I don't know who decides my kids belong there, but that's not my business. The children are numbered so that if any get

away they can be returned to the right class. Over the years, the variety of ways children are numbered by schools has increased dramatically, until it is hard to see the human beings plainly under the weight of numbers they carry.[4]

Kids learn to stay where they're put. They are treated as if they all mature at the same rate and should all fit the same mold of the model student.

Student. Teacher. Star of the Week. Valedictorian. School has a clear-cut box for everyone, making each person's position clear. Kids are encouraged to compete, seek status, and please adults, instead of learning together and collaborating.

What if we gave kids the freedom to define success for themselves?

Every kid is different. They have different talents and struggles, different goals and passions, and different ways they can contribute to the world.

What if we encouraged them to collaborate instead of compete for status? That way, they would learn that true success comes from people working together. Students would have the space they need to discover what makes them unique and they'd be able to offer the best version of themselves to their peers and the rest of society.

Lesson 3: Indifference

Schools teach kids not to invest too much in any one topic. Gatto says:

I teach children not to care too much about anything, even

though they want to make it appear that they do. How I do this is very subtle. I do it by demanding that they become totally involved in my lessons, jumping up and down in their seats with anticipation, competing vigorously with each other for my favor. It's heartwarming when they do that; it impresses everyone, even me. When I'm at my best, I plan lessons very carefully in order to produce this show of enthusiasm. But when the bell rings, I insist they drop whatever it is we have been doing and proceed quickly to the next workstation. They must turn on and off like a light switch.[5]

When a lesson, class period, or unit is finished, students are expected to stop studying that subject. No matter how much they liked it, they must move on to the next thing. I remember finally getting my third-graders excited about poetry—and then stopping them right after to move on to the next lesson.

How can I expect them to care about a topic when I'm forced to cut off their interest as soon as it sparks?

Kids internalize concepts best when using them to build relevant projects or solve real problems.

Students are treated like computers, expected to switch their attention to whatever we command them to do. It's dehumanizing and frustrating—and a huge drag on their productivity. It's also quite different from how life works.

You might be thinking, hold on, isn't context-switching and multitasking a valuable skill in the real world—the ability to be adaptable and switch between different tasks and skills at short notice? However, I struggle to find any research that supports this being a good thing. To the contrary, research suggests we are more effective, attentive, and productive when we focus.[6]

> **We should let kids follow their interests and empower them to dig into subjects that excite them.**

If you think about it, this fits with how real life works. Think about how much more deep knowledge you gain on a subject when you read a book, as opposed to scrolling through a list of disparate short topics on social media. And in the real world, people are rewarded for extreme focus on things they're passionate about. The person who jumps from topic to topic can't dive deep into problems that our society needs them to solve.

We should let kids follow their interests and empower them to dig into subjects that excite them. That's a much better way to prepare them to succeed as adults.

Lesson 4:
Emotional Dependency

Schools teach kids to rely on teachers to tell them how they should feel. As Gatto put it, "By stars and red checks, smiles and frowns, prizes, honors, and disgraces, I teach kids to surrender their will to the predestined chain of command."[7]

The traditional classroom makes each student feel the emotions that their teachers want them to feel. Consider a teacher's body language—it's one of our most powerful tools. *Warm* and *welcoming*, or *stern* and *closed off*.

Students are taught to feel shame when their teachers want them to feel shame, and pride when their teachers want them to feel pride. Their right to feel what's authentic to them is taken away.

What if we encourage kids to embrace their own emotions? What if we help them work through their feelings? Kids can't learn to regulate and manage their feelings—or build resilience!— when they're forced to mirror the emotions of someone else.

Lesson 5:
Intellectual Dependency

Schools take away the chance for kids to think for themselves and develop their *own* perspectives. Gatto states the issue well: "Good students wait for a teacher to tell them what to do. This is the most important lesson of them all: we must wait for other people, better trained than ourselves, to make the meanings of our lives."[8]

In school, kids have little room to develop their own ideas. Their intelligence is decided based on how well they parrot back to the teacher the ideologies of the school system. When kids do things their own way or ask hard questions, they're labeled as *troublemakers*.

But conforming and submitting to authority does not move society forward. It's the people who think for themselves who create progress.

Kids must formulate their own perspectives and practice evaluating their own ideas. We need more classrooms full of kids who practice divergent thinking and approach problems from new and unusual angles.

Lesson 6: Provisional Self-Esteem

Schools teach kids that their worth comes from what a professional thinks of them. Gatto wrote:

> Our world wouldn't survive a flood of confident people very long, so I teach that a kid's self-respect should depend on expert opinion. My kids are constantly evaluated and judged. A monthly report, impressive in its provision, is sent into a student's home to elicit approval or mark exactly, down to a single percentage point, how dissatisfied with the child a parent should be.[9]

Schools teach families to distrust their own judgment. Certified educators make parents feel as though they *don't have the right expertise*. Teachers become the judges of a child's worth, encouraged by strict school parameters to find flaw after flaw.

Instead, what if we taught kids to develop an inner measuring stick? What if we train them to be the captains of their own ship— the CEOs of their own lives?

After all, they will be the ones ultimately responsible for their choices, their learning, their behavior, and their accomplishments throughout life.

Authority figures will come and go with their different

opinions. It's only our own evaluation of our performance that ultimately lasts. The goal of teaching should be to help students develop that internal standard and use it to make good decisions.

Lesson 7:
Students Can't Hide

Schools put kids under the careful observation of authorities. Gatto says:

> I teach students that they are always watched, that each is under constant surveillance by me and my colleagues. There are no private spaces for children; there is no private time. Class change lasts exactly three hundred seconds to keep promiscuous fraternization at low levels. Students are encouraged to tattle on each other or even to tattle on their own parents.[10]

Kids have no privacy, no personal space, and few rights. Their parents are taught that autonomy is a bad thing. It's the seed of rebellion, damaging a student's proper development.

Instead, what if we gave kids a taste of adult freedom? As they grow up, shouldn't they experience more and more opportunities to do things on their own?

They need moments for privacy, chances to develop creative ideas, and a little bit of try, fail, and try again. Experimentation is critical for learning. If we're surveilling kids and their choices, how will they gain the confidence to try new things?

Gatto's point isn't that every kid experiences each of these problems, or that all teachers fall into every trap. He just wants us to open our eyes to the detrimental byproducts of our well-intentioned school system.

Teachers—our passionate, vocation-driven, hardworking allies—aren't to blame. But the incentives of school nudge them in the wrong direction. No matter how hard they resist, the system takes its toll and leads them toward counterproductive habits.

What if we encouraged kids to collaborate instead of compete for status?

When I was a teacher, I felt the force of this unhealthy system. I know I wasn't alone, as most teachers I know feel it too. For years, I saw how the system resists change. This is why I left to explore options outside of traditional school.

Schools are broken partly because they're so centralized, as most of them are run by the government. But most private schools use the same framework with the same dangerous lessons. Each flaw in the model flows out to impact nearly every kid across the globe.

The damage of these lessons doesn't stop in school. The model is also common among adult education and corporate training, perpetuating the same harmful characteristics. The seven dangerous lessons have become more or less "best practices." They've infiltrated our idea of learning, making us feel like we *can't learn* unless we're in a classroom with someone telling us what to do.

In the chapters ahead, I offer a different perspective. I explore alternative ways of learning that better match how we gain new knowledge and skills. And I'll lay out techniques that turn learning from boring and discouraging into exciting, creative, and challenging.

But before that, we need to dig a little deeper into *how* and *why* education went wrong.

In other words, we need to ask...

2

*How Did
We Get
Here?*

STARTED NOTICING THE problems with school when I watched my first group of students grow up. As they left my class and went from grade to grade, the spark of learning faded from their eyes. They stopped caring. Learning turned into a chore.

What went wrong?

I had hoped they would enjoy education *more* the older they got.

John Taylor Gatto helped me put words to the problems with school, but I was still puzzled. How did we end up with this system? Where did it come from?

I dove into the history of education, and what I found surprised me: the challenges we face in education have deep roots.

The History of Education: Prussia

Education used to be the job of parents, private tutors, and churches. But about 200 years ago, that started to change in a region of Germany called Prussia.[1] Government leaders decided they needed to take responsibility to educate children. They had just suffered a major loss: Napoleon's army had decisively beaten them and taken much of their land. As a result, Prussia decided to build an army of educated, loyal soldiers.

They never wanted to experience a defeat like that again.

The Prussian government designed the basics of our modern school system: specialized buildings, teacher certifications, standardized curriculum, extended school year, and mandated attendance. The goal was to train a generation of loyal, literate citizens prepared for war.

They taught 'academic freedom,' but it was limited by service to the state. As the philosopher Johann Gottlieb Fichte put it: "The citizens should be made able and willing to use their own minds to achieve higher goals in the framework of a future unified German nation state."[2]

The system worked. Prussia built one of the strongest fighting forces in the world. Their model spread across the world like wildfire, and set the stage for what we know today as *school*.[3]

EDUCATION TIMELINE

PRUSSIAN EDUCATION SYSTEM IS INTRODUCED

BEGINNING OF EDUCATION

TODAY

JOB OF PARENTS, TUTORS, & CHURCHES

JOB OF GOVERNMENT & MODERN SCHOOL SYSTEM

While the Prussian model served some good purposes—literacy rates skyrocketed[4]—it had a notable downside: it used education as a mask for indoctrination. The system was designed to build a loyal army that would win wars, with no intention to raise citizens who think for themselves.

The History of Education: The USA

By the time the 1950s rolled around, government leaders across the world saw education as essential to nation-building. Developing a loyal military was still a driving factor, but World War II revealed the importance of a nation's manufacturing capacity. The United States dominated because its factories and assembly lines could build more ships, tanks, guns, and bombs than its enemies.[5] As a result, the aim of school shifted from training lots of soldiers to training lots of managers to work in corporations and run factories.

The system was not designed to raise citizens who think for themselves.

And what's the best way to produce lots of educated managers? Put them on an assembly line as well! The factory model had worked for so many different things: food, cars, clothes, bullets, and so much more. Why not use it for education?

The United States led the next development in the history of education. The theme was standardization and efficiency.[6]

Group kids together by age. Put them all through the same curriculum. Hire specialized teachers for each subject. Ring bells to move them from class to class. Make the school day long to maximize output. Reduce talking and playing to eliminate waste. Anyone who didn't fit the mold was labeled defective.

This model gained full momentum in the 1960s, when we started using modern standardized tests to evaluate students.[7] These tests functioned as a way to track quality control, similar to how manufacturers check whether a car works as it should. Tests were meant to give administrators confidence that their system worked—and kept schools accountable.

It's hard to find the benefits of the modern school system in the United States. In over 50 years, standardized test scores have only improved by a small margin.[8] You would expect that schools designed to create effective factory managers would advance a nation's productivity and standard of living, but the rate of improvement since the 1970s has actually declined.[9]

Today, over half of Americans can't read beyond a sixth-grade level.[10] Confidence in public schools is near all-time lows, right below government and big business.[11] Our most famous innovators, including Bill Gates, Steve Jobs, Mark Zuckerberg, Oprah Winfrey, and Elon Musk, are famous for *dropping out* of their degree programs. Their stories are so powerful because they highlight something every student feels: what's the point of school?

The Problems with Instruction-Based Learning and the Lego Analogy

As we've seen, the history of education has led to a system of learning that prioritizes state and government needs instead of individual learning. But what exactly is its core defect? What's at the heart of the problem? We can tease out the primary issue through an analogy with the toy company Lego.

Lego used to come in all colors and sizes, inside a large box with no instructions. The blocks could become a village, a robot, or a dinosaur. Kids could make whatever they wanted in whatever manner they wanted. They went through the process *on their own*.

To boost sales, the company decided to try another approach: selling Lego kits.[12] Kits came with instructions plus a picture of what the end product should look like: a bouquet of flowers, a Harry Potter classroom, or a Transformer.

Parents have bought these Lego kits like crazy: over 220 million sets are sold worldwide each year.[13] But here's the problem: the kits removed the opportunity for kids to solve problems for themselves.[14]

As cognitive scientist Derek Cabrera points out, the adults at Lego who design the kits are the ones solving problems. Kids end up mimicking the picture on the box.[15]

Sure, the results look great (and make parents proud!), but Lego kits end up only teaching kids to follow instructions, leaving little room for independent thinking.

The Lego example is a sign of the limits of our education system. As author and entrepreneur Seth Godin says, "Lego isn't the problem, but it is a symptom of something seriously amiss."[16]

> When we over-instruct and specify each step of the learning process, we limit kids' agency and creativity.

We're treating kids like they need adults to solve their problems. Teachers and administrators over-engineer lesson plans and curriculums while students are told to follow directions and formulas. The adults who create the lesson plans do the problem-solving, while kids end up bored and resentful.

When we specify exactly what a final assignment should look like, we underestimate students' ability to think deeply. When we over-instruct and specify each step of the learning process, we limit kids' agency and creativity. Most importantly, we leave students ill-equipped to handle the difficult, ambiguous problems they will face as adults.

"

Kids are naturals at figuring things out if we let them be. They might be confused and unsure at first, but these are good, motivating feelings that encourage them to break molds and reach their full potential.

"

Our education system is designed around instruction-based methods. This is a suboptimal way of learning with a number of significant problems:

First, kids get fewer opportunities for elastic thinking. Elastic thinking is when we discover new perspectives by letting our minds wander through problems. It's critical for making new discoveries and finding creative solutions. When we give kids instructions, we eliminate the chance for them to stumble on new, bold ideas. See chapter 19 for more on this topic.

Second, they experience less excitement around learning. When we give kids specific instructions, we're killing their curiosity. They have little chance to feel excited to learn because all the mystery from the problem has been removed. Their motivation dwindles because they have no chance to make a genuine contribution. Everything has already been solved for them.

Third, they develop lower self-esteem. Kids start to think that they *need* instructions to solve problems. They don't feel empowered to chart new territory or tackle difficult challenges. As a result, their sense of self-worth plummets. They're scared to strike out on their own because they're afraid of failure.

Instructions may boost short-term performance. Kids might earn better grades when all the specifics are laid out for them to follow. But at what cost? Is a higher GPA really worth kids losing their creative thinking, motivation, and self-worth in the process?

Learning Without Instructions

Scripted lesson plans and paint-by-numbers thinking are not good enough. We need to go back to the original Lego philosophy—provide a box of building blocks, then get out of the way and let kids create.

Kids are naturals at figuring things out if we *let them be*. They might be confused and unsure at first, but these are good, motivating feelings that encourage them to break molds and reach their full potential.

> We need to provide a box of building blocks, then get out of the way and let kids create.

When adults stop over-instructing, kids start thinking creatively and independently. As we ask kids to put more of themselves into learning, they'll rise to the challenge and become more engaged and better prepared.

After all, life doesn't come with an instruction booklet. It's messy and unpredictable. To prepare kids for the real world, we need to give space for their imagination to shine. That means taking away instructions and making room for problem-solving.

INSTRUCTIONS

As we've seen, the history of education has led us to an instruction-based model of learning. Teachers are responsible for solving problems. It's the job of students to simply follow directions. As a result, kids become deeply disengaged. School takes away the opportunity for children to get excited about solving hard problems for themselves.

So, how does an education system respond when kids lose interest? It creates extrinsic incentives designed to motivate students and coerce them to participate.

To see how, let's look at...

3

How Tests and Rewards Go Wrong

W E HAVE RESORTED to a lot of nonsense in the name of "accountability."

Standardized tests were intended to measure learning, but the one thing they measure for sure is a kid's ability at taking tests.

Schools compete on standardized test results to remain relevant, and teachers risk losing their jobs if their students don't perform. No wonder these tests have become the most important part of the year!

You wouldn't believe what goes on in school during standardized test season. Teachers drop everything to get in a few last-minute prep sessions. The system incentivizes teachers to do whatever is necessary to bump up their students' results. Just imagine the unintended consequences. In 2015, for example, 11 educators in Atlanta, Georgia were convicted of racketeering after years of cheating.[1]

Of course, racketeering is an extreme example of how tests go wrong. Less attention-grabbing, but more widespread, is the problem of how the tests encourage poor behavior in smaller (but still significant) ways. Consider how tests incentivize teachers to rely on short-term rewards ("Pizza party if we nail the MAP tests!") that reduce long-term student engagement.

In this chapter, we will talk about the problems with traditional standardized tests and the extrinsic motivators schools often use to improve test results. I'll also suggest better ways to measure the progress of students and motivate them to experience genuine learning.

The Origin of Standardized Tests

About 100 years ago, we started using standardized tests to assess student progress and achievement. Scientists did lots of research to ensure tests measured intelligence and skills like math, reading, and writing.[2]

For decades, standardized tests gave kids and parents some useful information. To this day, they provide a baseline measurement of kids' academic knowledge and capabilities.

But things started to change in the late 1960s.[3] Standardized tests started gaining importance within the system. Fast forward to today and these tests have taken a whole 'nother level of importance.

The one thing tests measure for sure is a kid's ability at taking tests.

Kids repeat grades, enter gifted programs, earn scholarships, and get into college, all based on standardized test scores. Teachers lose their jobs and public schools lose funding when students don't perform on these tests.

Standardized tests are no longer just assessments. They've become the whole point of our education system.

Schools have fallen victim to Campbell's Law, which says that measurements destroy learning when they're set up as a goal.[4]

The Problem with Standardized Tests

Standardized tests have contributed to the decline of our education system in multiple ways:

First, they create poor learning environments. Kids learn best when they follow their interests and passions, but teachers today can't give kids this freedom. They might not test on grade level! Kids spend much of the year in test prep instead of engaging in authentic learning experiences.

Second, tests can compromise the mental health of students. Test anxiety is real. As a teacher, I saw countless kids bite their nails to the quick and double over from stomach pain. Test anxiety affects performance and also reduces kids' interest in learning, or taking on challenging tasks.[5]

Third, tests do not reflect whether a kid will succeed in the real world. High scores may provide some insight into academic talent, but most of all, they measure a student's test-taking ability. This skill is obviously not sufficient to do well as an adult! What's more, mediocre scores do not mean students can't be successful. Actress Scarlett Johansson, President Bill Clinton, and baseball player Alex Rodriguez have led successful careers, even though they didn't score well on the SAT. Why? Because the real world rewards people who know how to learn, solve problems, and perform, not people who are good at taking tests.

Fourth, tests incentivize corrupt institutions. Kids, parents, teachers, schools, districts, and even states have been caught falsifying results. Even worse, some schools end up forcing out *weak* students to raise their average scores. Putting standardized testing on a pedestal creates bad incentives for all involved.[6]

In sum, tests create bad incentives when set up as goals.

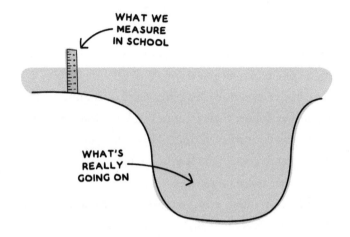

When set up as goals, standardized tests cause education to go wrong. But the solution isn't to ban assessments. We need ways to track student progress and keep schools accountable while avoiding the negative side effects of standardized testing.

A Better Way Forward

What if the solution is to *lower the stakes* and *open up the options*?

By *lowering the stakes*, I mean making standardized tests less important.

Kids experience genuine learning when exploring, creating, and tinkering with things—when they're relaxed, not worried about being judged. Standardized tests get in the way of this authentic kind of learning when the stakes are too high. Perhaps it's time to consider lowering their priority.

By *opening up the options*, I mean broadening the methods by which we measure progress. As one principal put it:

> Amongst the students who will be sitting for the exams is an artist, who doesn't need to understand Math... There is an entrepreneur, who doesn't care about History or English literature... There is a musician, whose Chemistry marks won't matter.[7]

What if these kids had other ways to show their skills and knowledge? Standardized test results hardly represent any of these kids' true potential.

Homeschoolers, for example, submit portfolios to their local Board of Education. A portfolio might include art, short stories, business plans, and other work. What if every kid had the opportunity to show what they know?

Ultimately, assessments should aim to give feedback to kids so they can improve. That means we need methods to evaluate them that match their particular gifts and goals. Combining exams with portfolios could be a promising solution.

The value of measuring student progress in multiple ways is that we don't need to motivate kids to perform. Empowering them to show what they've learned *in a way that suits their style* is enough of an incentive.

It's different when it's all about standardized tests. Kids feel set up for failure, and they miss the bigger picture of *learning*. They focus on memorization, just so they can pass the test.

Amid this swarm of bad incentives for all involved, teachers resort to the problematic use of *extrinsic* rewards.

I resisted this temptation with my students—and the results were surprising.

Rewards in My Classroom

When I was a teacher, one of my goals every year was to create a classroom that could run itself. I didn't want kids to engage and learn because I was hovering over them. I wanted them to be self-motivated.

My co-workers couldn't figure out how I was doing it. They would use every classroom-management technique in the book. Treasure boxes filled with prizes for good behavior. "Good work!" coupons kids could exchange for goodies. Star-shaped stickers that added up to extra recess time.

But for some reason, nothing seemed to work. No matter what they tried, their classrooms would devolve into chaos as soon as they left.

I said "no" to rewards. You wouldn't find any of these things in my classroom. Still, kids stayed engaged for hours each day, diving into their favorite subjects.

I found that rewards actually hurt engagement over the long run.

Extrinsic motivators like rewards may help kids reach some short-term academic benchmarks or behavior goals, but they distract us from the ultimate goal of raising self-directed, lifelong learners.

The Problem with Extrinsic Motivators

Extrinsic motivators are common in most classrooms and homes. *We reward kids when they do as they are told or remove privileges when they don't.*

The logic behind extrinsic motivators is intuitive. A behavior that is rewarded or punished is more or less likely to be repeated. Most of the time, these work—and rather quickly. Kids who are promised a reward will often immediately change their behavior or decide to engage.

> How can we raise self-directed learners if we get them into the habit of expecting a reward for doing the right thing?

But there are a few problems with this approach:

First, rewards don't work forever.

There is a limit to how many rewards we can promise and give—after some time, these rewards become repetitive and boring. Once the short-term benefit of a reward ends, the child's motivation fades.

Second, what are we teaching our children when we promise a reward to get them to do something?

We're telling them that they should care about what they'll get instead of enjoying the learning process. They do things for the reward or to avoid punishment, rather than for the sake of learning itself.

How can we raise self-directed learners if we get kids into the habit of expecting a reward for doing the right thing?

The key is in *intrinsic* motivation.

EXTRINSIC MOTIVATION

INTRINSIC MOTIVATION

How to Unlock Intrinsic Motivation

We all learn best when we're intrinsically motivated.

As author Daniel Pink says, "The secret to high performance isn't rewards and punishments, but that unseen intrinsic drive—the drive to do things for their own sake. The drive to do things 'cause they matter."[8]

What's true of adults is also true of kids. They learn to love learning when they engage in activities driven by their curiosity and inner desire to explore. Kids who *understand* the value of what they are doing or learning stop caring about extrinsic rewards.

Here are five things I did to motivate my students intrinsically that you can try with your kids:

First, give kids choices and make them feel accountable. Giving children choices and responsibilities builds a sense of excitement, accountability, and purpose.

I provided students with choices on *what* and *how* they learned.

Kids learn to love learning when they engage in activities driven by their curiosity and inner desire to explore.

Even simple choices, like picking which book to read, who to work with, or where to sit, make children feel empowered. I also found that kids who are given choices are more prone to finding time outside of school to continue learning on their own—a crucial trait of self-directed learners.

I gave students specific classroom *jobs* that made them feel accountable. I catered jobs to their personality and inclinations. For example, my hyperactive students ran classroom errands. The most likely to misbehave became my teacher helpers.

It worked like magic! The hyperactive students were able to release energy throughout the day. The "troublemakers" felt special because they had the most important classroom jobs, so they made the effort to set a positive example. They raised to the level of expectation.

Every student knew that completing their jobs would help their classmates and teacher. They took their responsibilities seriously because they understood that our classroom worked best when everyone contributed.

Second, involve kids when making decisions. Children who perceive they are in control are more likely to engage in their learning.

My students and I had discussions about social and behavioral expectations for our classroom, and we came up with rules and logical consequences that they understood and accepted.

These agreements were reached together, so they made sense to everyone. For example, the rule "You break it, you fix it" applied to both classroom supplies and other people's feelings. Students were responsible for fixing any problem or mess they created. Because they had a voice and influence over these issues, they were more likely to take them seriously.

As author Polina Pompliano points out, parents can engage kids in decisions by conducting *family meetings*. She writes:

> Struggling to implement rules in your household? Instead of taking a top-down approach, try a bottom-up approach. For instance, if you want to limit the time your kids spend in front of a screen, call a family meeting and tell them you want them to come up with fair rules. Allow your kids to be part of the rule-making process.[9]

When we involve children in decisions, they begin to understand the reasons behind our choices and are more likely to cooperate.

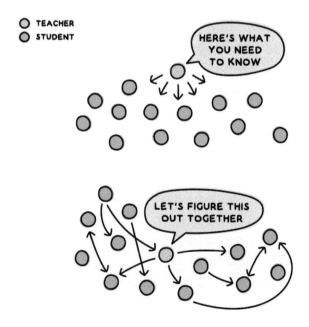

Kids who *understand* the value of what they are doing or learning stop caring about extrinsic rewards.

Third, be specific with feedback and questions. Children, like adults, seek recognition for their accomplishments and benefit from knowing how they are doing. We can recognize their positive efforts and encourage them to build on their strengths by giving them specific feedback.

When offering words of encouragement, we need to be specific so that children know exactly what they are doing well. Don't just say, "Good work!" Good work on what?

Similarly, resist using generic praises such as "Well done!" or "That's amazing!" Try asking questions about their process instead. Be curious about the *how* rather than praising the *what*. Here are some examples:

- "How did you think to make that? What was your favorite part? Will you tell me more about it?"
- "I saw the tower you were building fell down, and instead of getting frustrated, you took a deep breath and built it again. That was really cool to watch."
- "Wow, you scored a goal! How did that feel? Your enthusiasm for soccer is contagious."

As a rule of thumb, recognize effort, not ability, and recognize ethics over achievement. Recognize the learning process, not the outcome. Recognize curiosity, perseverance, and a growth mindset over the completion of tasks.

It's equally important to ask good questions when talking with our kids. When we ask broad questions, like "How was your day in school today?" we are likely to get broad answers, like "Good" or "Fine." Instead, try asking more specific questions, like "What was one high and one low from your day?" (Side note: this works great with spouses too!)

Fourth, have frequent "why" conversations. Kids demand to know the meaning and relevance of what they're doing and learning. And rightly so!

As author Malcolm Gladwell wrote, "Hard work is a prison sentence only if it does not have meaning." Kids stay engaged and enjoy the process when they understand the *why* behind what we encourage them to do.

I framed my classroom lessons in ways that were relevant to my students' preferences, and provided context for why each topic was important.

I noticed that children feel satisfied when engaging in meaningful dialogue. They love nurturing their curiosity and learning about *adult* decisions. The conversations I had with my students about the importance of certain tasks and behaviors brought meaning to their learning and made them want to engage more.

> Kids feel satisfied when engaging in meaningful dialogue, and love learning about *adult* decisions.

Fifth, make fun a priority. Children who have fun learn more and behave better than those who don't. Similarly, when children enjoy what they are doing, they are more likely to keep doing it.

Having fun was a top priority in my class. I spent time thinking of what got me excited as a child and the things that made me feel valued and engaged, and tried to replicate them.

I made sure children were excited to be part of our classroom. I realized that my job wasn't to teach kids how to multiply or subtract: my priority was to instill in them a *love for learning*.

I worked hard to bring fun to everything we did by incorporating humor and engaging in fun activities for the sake of having fun. Although my classroom had appealing features that made it unique, none were tied to student achievement or positive behavior. This sent the message that learning and fun can go together—that learning and fun *should* go together.

**MOTIVATION
WHEN I'M FORCED
TO DO SOMETHING**

**MOTIVATION
WHEN I CHOOSE
TO DO SOMETHING**

While motivating kids intrinsically is harder, it's worth the time and effort. After all, instilling in children a love for learning is the most valuable gift we can give them.

> Instilling in kids a love for learning is the most valuable gift we can give them.

Sadly, the educational system does not share this conviction. It's simply not designed to captivate kids with the joy of learning. It relies on extrinsic motivators and short-term rewards, leading to a much less desired result: compliance.

School focuses on well-run classrooms, not creativity, curiosity, or problem-solving. It ends up giving kids ideas on what success looks like that conflict with their natural development as driven lifelong learners.

To help kids achieve genuine success in the real world, we need to teach them...

4

---

*Lessons
to Unlearn
from School*

UTHOR ALVIN TOFFLER once wrote, "The illiterate of the 21st century will not be those who cannot read and write, but those who cannot learn, unlearn and relearn."[1]

Unlearning is the skill of recognizing our deeply held beliefs about something and realizing that the inverse might actually be true. Unlearning is especially important for the things we're taught in school. As we've discussed over the past few chapters, our education system wasn't always designed with the best at heart for kids.

In this chapter, we will look at a series of lessons taught in school that kids would do better not believing. Teachers convey these lessons with the best of intentions, but they're simply not true. In fact, as we will see, they're often flat-out wrong. Kids would do better to do the *opposite* of these lessons taught in school.

Five Lessons to Unlearn

First, we need to help kids unlearn *fearing mistakes*. In school, kids lose points for mistakes. In the real world, mistakes are how we learn the most.

Success in school comes from getting high marks on tests. And students don't get high marks on tests if they make mistakes.

Mistakes in school are penalized, frowned upon, and associated with failure. As a result, kids learn to fear them.

There are two big problems with this. First, being scared of making mistakes *is* a mistake. Think about it. Growing up means making many mistakes. It's how people learn and improve. It's how people understand what works and what doesn't. The most successful people in the real world are comfortable with making (and handling) mistakes. As we discuss in chapter 17, failure isn't something we should teach children to avoid. It's an art that we should help them master.

Unlearn: Fearing mistakes.

Relearn: Getting comfortable with mistakes and learning from them.

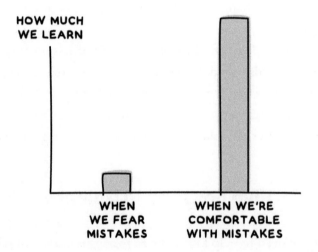

Second, kids need to unlearn *fitting in*. In school, students are rewarded for coloring inside the lines. In the real world, they're rewarded for thinking outside the box.

Schools use one-size-fits-all tactics to try to put kids into a box. They all learn the same things, in the same way, at the same time and pace. They are rewarded for pursuing paths according to someone else's rules. They are taught to compare themselves to others and strive to be better rather than different. They learn to conform. They learn to fit in.

But the real world rewards people who think and act independently: those who think outside the box and stand out from the norm. Successful people in the real world carve their own paths. They develop *range*, a broad base of general knowledge and experiences, which give them the opportunity to find their unique talents and specific knowledge. We take a deep dive into this topic in chapter 16.

Unlearn: Striving to fit in.

Relearn: Breaking from the pack, finding what makes you different, and creating something legendary.

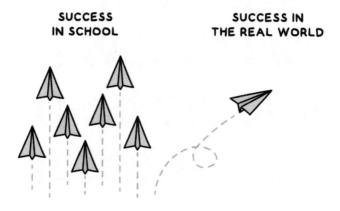

SUCCESS IN SCHOOL

SUCCESS IN THE REAL WORLD

> **Failure isn't something we should teach children to avoid. It's an art that we should help them master.**

Third, they need to unlearn *waiting for instructions*. In school, we have to wait for instructions and do as we are told. In the real world, we have to figure things out for ourselves.

In school, we have to wait for teachers to tell us what to learn and how to learn it. We learn to stay put and not get ahead of ourselves. We depend on someone telling us what to do.

Waiting for instructions doesn't play well in the real world. Employers don't like to hire people who need to be told what to do all the time. To succeed in the real world, we need to test ideas until we figure things out. The world rewards those who are proactive and independent—those who can problem-solve and have the initiative to figure things out. These are the kinds of people who respond to confusion with curiosity, not frustration, as we will see in chapter 10.

Unlearn: Waiting for instructions.

Relearn: Trying > Failing > Learning > Refining > Repeating until you figure things out.

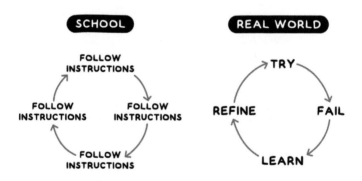

Fourth, kids need to unlearn *learning "just in case."* In school, we learn things *just in case* we need them later. In the real world, we learn specific things when the need arises.

School teaches us all sorts of things from a fixed curriculum, hoping that some things will be useful later. We learn long division "just in case" we don't have a phone with us. We memorize the periodic table "just in case" we ever need to recite it (*what?*). We learn to compare triangles "just in case" it comes in handy.[2]

> The world rewards those who can problem-solve and have the initiative to figure things out.

In the real world, those who succeed are the ones who have mastered how to teach themselves. They're prepared for any problem they might face, not because they've memorized all the answers just in case they ever need them, but because they know how to find answers when they need them. When they do use memorization, they only focus on what's meaningful and genuinely important, not trivia that's easy to google, as we cover in chapter 8. That's because they're skilled at learning *on demand*.

Unlearn: Learning "just in case."
Relearn: Learning "on demand."

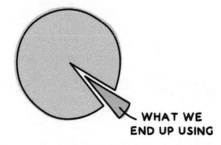

**WHAT WE LEARN
IN SCHOOL**

**WHAT WE
END UP USING**

Fifth, we need to help kids unlearn *the fear of questioning authority*. In school, students learn to not question authority. In the real world, we should question everything.

Kids learn in school not to challenge their teachers. Those who question or have different opinions are labeled as the "difficult ones." Students get used to accepting answers like "because I said so" or "because that's how we do things here."

> If we don't ask questions, we get stuck with the status quo. When we question things, we innovate.

In the real world, questioning things helps us develop opinions and come up with our own ideas. If we don't ask questions, we get stuck with the status quo. When we question things, we innovate.

We excel when we work on projects of our own—not projects that we're forced to do. In the next chapter, we unpack this idea further, focusing on how ownership empowers us to take responsibility and pursue our own unique ideas.

Unlearn: Don't ask too many questions.

Relearn: It's ok to question everything.

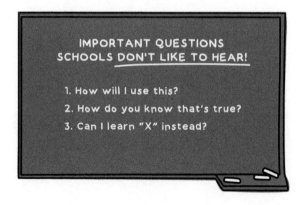

IMPORTANT QUESTIONS
SCHOOLS DON'T LIKE TO HEAR!

1. How will I use this?
2. How do you know that's true?
3. Can I learn "X" instead?

We can make a big difference by helping kids unlearn the unhelpful lessons taught in school. Unfortunately, these lessons live in the bones of our education system. They're principles that run through nearly every classroom. As a result, kids don't learn how to take risks, stand out, solve problems for themselves, learn to learn anything, and ask hard questions.

Instead, kids learn how to play...

5

The Game of School

HUMANS ARE DESIGNED, by nature, to learn. We learn through self-directed play, exploration, and trial and error. We learn by digging deep into our interests, making things, and reflecting on the impact and consequences of our actions. These are instincts. They come automatically to us.

The problem is that formal school does not match the usual way humans learn.

In this chapter, we discuss how school has taken learning out of its natural context and put it into an institutional framework. We also talk about the value of breaking out of the game of school and playing, instead, *the learning game*.

Getting Good at the Game of School

Think about your own school experience. How much of the learning that happened in school stuck over the years? I'm guessing very little.

That's because the learning that occurs in formal schooling is mostly an *imitation of learning*.

LEARN FOR A TEST AND LESSONS FADE

Adults have a hard time noticing when kids imitate learning because kids are good at it. Kids are smart, adaptable, and quick at catching on to things. They've figured out how to navigate a flawed system by appearing diligent and attentive. In other words, they've learned to play the game of school.

Humans are designed, by nature, to learn.

The game of school is easy to master. Kids quickly pick up on what a successful student looks like. They try to look like they're paying attention in class, raise their hand every few minutes, and turn in homework on time. They try to get away with doing as little as possible to pass the test so they can get school out of the way and head off to do what really matters to them.

Can we blame them?

With the framework we've created for school, what incentives do kids have to value real learning over grades?

In fact, they're incentivized to go through the motions and check all the boxes, even when they haven't fully grasped a topic. Students who fall behind aren't the ones who learn the least. They're the ones who couldn't keep up with the pace of the class. As a result, the average student figures out how to graduate from school, but not how to learn the knowledge and skills they need to succeed in life.

Instead of the game of school, we need to help kids master a different game—one that plays to their strengths and gives them a competitive advantage in life.

The Learning Game

Not every student falls into the game of school. Some of them recognize the harmful pattern and resist the pressures to conform.

We need to help kids master a different game— one that plays to their strengths and gives them a competitive advantage in life.

Instead of engaging in the game of school, they play the game that really matters: the game of learning.

These kids often look like rebels. They question assignments, stretch the rules of projects, and may choose to focus on one or a few subjects. They might not always earn the highest grades, but it doesn't bother them. They're not playing school to get a high GPA. They're in the business of learning—a much more powerful and lasting reward for their efforts.

The game that really matters is the game of learning.

These kids succeed in life not only because they learn more. They succeed also because they figured out how to get the most out of life. They're not bound by typical rules. They're not in the game of performing like everyone else. They're choosing to play their own game by thinking at a higher level and working on the things they find fulfilling. These kids are better equipped to contribute to the world because they understand what they uniquely bring to the table.

We shouldn't look down on these kids. Instead, we should encourage them—and try to become more like them! No matter what we do in life, we'll do it better if we can break out of the ordinary mold and tilt the tables in our favor. That's the key to success.

But how do we figure out the game of learning? How do we teach ourselves and our kids the skill of flipping the script and approaching problems from different angles?

To answer these questions, we need to take a step back. We need to reexamine our assumptions about how education works. We need to rethink long-held beliefs about not only school but also the entire process of how we gain knowledge and skills.

In short, we need to look at...

How
Kids
Learn

———————

6

*Learning
to Love
Learning*

WHEN WE TELL kids to put away the guitar, or stop diving into vintage fashion, and get back to "real work" (that is, schoolwork), we're telling them that learning and joy are separate.

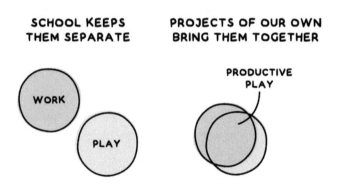

SCHOOL KEEPS
THEM SEPARATE

PROJECTS OF OUR OWN
BRING THEM TOGETHER

PRODUCTIVE
PLAY

WORK

PLAY

It's common to keep work and play separate. Personal projects often look like play, and we tend to think that play and learning shouldn't overlap. The same goes for adults: hobbies are for after you punch out for the day.

But by keeping hobbies on the sidelines, we miss a key opportunity to learn from diving into projects of our own.

In this chapter, we will discuss how personal projects spark genuine learning in children. We'll also talk about how having agency over their work helps them see things from different angles and discover new possibilities.

Projects of Our Own

We feel most ourselves when we work on projects of our own. These projects may not give us constant satisfaction (every writer puzzles over their pages), but they are where we feel the most engaged and uninhibited.

The same applies to kids. When kids work on projects of their own, they set aside everything but the task at hand. They're focused on thinking, learning, and doing. It's hard work, but hard work they choose *voluntarily*.

Let's use investor Paul Graham's example of building treehouses.[1]

At a first glance, the project may seem like nothing more than play. But when building a treehouse, kids learn about all sorts of things like math, engineering, and teamwork. They are thinking, making plans, and solving problems. Most importantly, they are highly engaged in the experience because they get to direct and manage their learning *on their own*.

In other words, projects of their own create the perfect conditions for genuine learning.

SITTING IN THE CLASSROOM...   ...LEARNING IN THE REAL WORLD

Yet in school, we continue to treat voluntary projects as different from real work. We label core topics as "curriculum" and fun ones as "extracurricular." We make kids believe that the path to success is through schoolwork and fail to emphasize that by working on projects of their own, they also engage in real and useful learning.

As Paul Graham writes:

It's a bit sad to think of all the high school kids turning their backs on building treehouses and sitting in class dutifully learning about Darwin or Newton to pass some exam, when the work that made Darwin and Newton famous was actually closer in spirit to building treehouses than studying for exams.[2]

Real learning happens when we work intensely on things that matter to us—and no one gets this better than kids. That's why they drag their feet as they walk to school in the fall and sprint away in the summer.

Imagine if school revolved around projects students got to choose—not curriculums, quotas, or tasks. Wouldn't kids be more engaged? Wouldn't this lead them to love school and learning?

A wonderful 11-year-old interviewed me for his podcast, Kids Learn Careers. Every week, he talks with a different person about their job so other kids can learn about the career options in today's world. I was fascinated by his passion and how much time and effort he has put into this project. Instead of viewing this podcast as just another after-school activity, his parents helped him see it as an opportunity to create value.

Many famous scientists, writers, artists, and entrepreneurs succeeded not because they were good in school, but because they allowed their projects outside of school to consume them.

Mark Zuckerberg dropped out of college to work on his platform for student networking called Facebook. Elon Musk turned down a Stanford PhD program to build Zip2, his first company. Jeni Britton Bauer quit her fine arts degree to start the wildly successful Jeni's Splendid Ice Creams chain. In her words: "I just walked out, left all my art supplies there, and rode my bike home to go make ice cream."[3] Zuckerberg, Musk, and Britton Bauer may seem like exceptions— and that shows how rarely people get the freedom to take seriously the project they care about most.

> Real learning happens when we work intensely on things that matter to us—and no one gets this better than kids.

Let's normalize encouraging kids to work on projects of their own. Let's create the conditions for healthy obsessions to happen. Let's applaud kids for pursuing their curiosities. Let's make them feel like they're learning when it could seem like they're playing. Because they *are* learning, and they're also *learning to love learning*.

How Learning to Love Learning Sparks Innovation

Young kids and innovators share an important trait: what everyone else takes for granted, they see as new and ripe with opportunity.

To be a successful scientist, for example, you need to discover things that others haven't noticed. To start a successful company, you need to go after something that others haven't figured out.

As Paul Graham says, it's not enough to be correct. We must also be novel.[4]

We're born with a natural ability to think independently, but school trains it out of us. We're taught to strive for correctness and social approval instead of novelty. We're taught that if everyone agrees, the idea must be right, even if it's not useful or new.

When kids get to work on their own voluntary projects, they get the opportunity to cultivate novel approaches to problems. They're free to do things their way, no matter what a teacher or "best practices" say. They're free to pursue strategies and tactics that might look crazy to everyone else but make perfect sense to them.

But what I've come to realize is that projects of their own allow kids to cultivate innovative ideas because that's when they experience moments of *vuja de*.

Déjà vu occurs when we encounter something new, but it feels as if we've seen it before. Vuja de is the reverse. As Adam Grant says, "We face something familiar, but we see it with a fresh perspective that enables us to gain new insights into old problems."[5]

Consider the founders of Warby Parker, an American online retailer of prescription glasses and sunglasses.[6] For decades, everyone assumed glasses had to be expensive. Paying exorbitant prices for eyewear was the familiar default. Then, a few friends took a step back and asked the hard question:

"Why?"

With a little investigation, they uncovered a monopoly. One company owned LensCrafters, Pearle Vision, Ray-Ban, and Oakley, and the licenses for Chanel and Prada. This allowed them and their middlemen to charge extremely high prices.[7] Customers didn't have other options.

Once the friends identified the problem, the solution was clear. They needed to own the whole process, from glasses design and eye exams to distribution (stores and web). This allowed them to cut out all the middlemen and pass savings on to customers.

The founders of Warby Parker used a vuja de mindset.

They looked at a familiar situation from a fresh perspective. They questioned the default and built a $3 billion business in the process.[8]

Vuja de is one of the secrets to creative innovation in business, life, and everything else. It comes naturally to kids, but adults often squelch it.

How can we flip the script and encourage vuja de instead?

How to Encourage Vuja De

Here are four ways to encourage vuja de in kids:

First, cultivate an attitude of skepticism. When kids resist being told what to think, we often mistake it as a negative quality, when in reality it's the opposite. We should encourage this quest, not penalize it.

Teach your kids not to let anything into their head unexamined. Encourage them to ask questions like:

- "Is what that person just said true?"
- "How do I know that it is true?"
- "Who is telling the story and what are their motives?"

Another important aspect of being a skeptic is determining biases, starting with our own. We can help kids become aware of their own biases by asking them questions like:

- "What makes you think this way? What assumptions have you based your claim upon?"
- "What do you hope will be true?"
- "What facts or research support your ideas?"

A great family activity for this is to have a weekly myth-busting discussion at dinner.

Part of being a good skeptic is learning to play the devil's advocate. Invite kids to take a position they don't necessarily agree with, just for the sake of argument. Frame this habit as something positive—an exciting quest for novelty—rather than as something combative.

> Vuja de is one of the secrets to creative innovation in business, life, and everything else.

Second, help kids step back and observe from a distance. When we step back and reexamine something, we suddenly feel like we're seeing it for the first time. I love this quote by author Warren Berger:

> We're seeing essentially the same realities and situations. But with more distance, a bigger picture comes into view. We may now be able to see the overall context; we might notice the patterns and relationships between things we'd previously thought of as separate.[9]

We should try to help kids have the same experience. The problem is that in school, we move too quickly from one thing to another. Students rarely have time to linger and digest what they are learning.

Here are a few ways kids can practice stepping back and observing from a distance:

- Having someone read their piece of writing out loud to them.
- Rewriting a story from another character's point of view (perhaps the villain).
- Editing their writing from a different device, maybe a keyboard, phone, tablet, or with pen and paper.

> **Let's create the conditions for healthy obsessions to happen. Let's make kids feel like they're learning when it could seem like they're playing. Because they are learning, and they're also learning to love learning.**

- Trying to find another way to solve the same math problem.
- Coming back to something they read a few days (or even weeks) ago to see how their thinking has changed.
- Stepping away from a jigsaw puzzle and looking at it from a different angle.

Third, encourage kids to reject the defaults. When we reject the defaults, we start to notice inconsistencies, outdated methods, and overlooked opportunities. The sooner kids learn this habit, the better. As Adam Grant says:

Teach your kids it's okay to inquire and want more evidence before accepting a claim as true.

> The hallmark of originality is rejecting the default and exploring whether a better option exists. The starting point is curiosity: pondering why the default exists in the first place.[10]

Teach your kids it's okay to inquire and want more evidence before accepting a claim as true.

Cherish the "Why?" questions—it's kids' way of thinking from first principles. They ask "Why?" a lot because they're trying to understand how things work. They're trying to deconstruct what's thrown at them to decide if it makes sense. They're trying to think for themselves.

Fourth, ask deeper questions about what kids notice. When we ask conventional questions, we get conventional answers. It's worth the time to stop and push ourselves and our children to dig deeper. Invite kids to ask themselves questions like:

- "How strong is the evidence?"
- "Does this evidence come from a solid source?"

- "Is there an agenda behind it?"
- "What am I not being told?"
- "What information or details are missing?"
- "What is the opposing view?"
- "Which of the conflicting views has more evidence behind it?"

In the words of author Bob Sutton:

This means thinking of things that are usually assumed to be negative as positive, and vice versa. It can mean reversing assumptions about cause and effect, or what matters most versus least. It means not traveling through life on automatic pilot.[11]

Kids engage in deep learning when they pursue projects of their own. They get the opportunity to see things from a different perspective and use their own techniques. It's an exciting way to learn because kids get to bring themselves into the equation. They learn not only to enjoy their projects, but also to love the act of learning itself.

Cherish the "Why?" questions—it's kids' way of thinking from first principles.

They can also learn in another way that's just as exciting: from the unique ideas of other people. Kids can study other people's discoveries, copy some of their tactics, and integrate others' insights into their own work.

To see how, let's dive into…

7

Story-Driven Learning

WALK INTO A typical classroom today. You'll probably find a teacher lecturing about facts, figures, and formulas.

We treat kids like computers.

We give them rules and information, and if they're functioning properly, they'll process the data and spit out the right answer. Kids who struggle must have bugs in their system.

Humans are great at logic and math. But it's not the natural way we learn. We weren't designed in a laboratory to follow code. We evolved to learn by mimicking people from stories.

In this chapter, we'll look at how stories are powerful tools for learning. They make concepts concrete and offer us practical examples of people we can emulate. They make abstract theories, formulas, and numbers more meaningful to us by using a tactic as old as the human race itself.

Just look at the cave drawings of our ancestors. Every once in a while, you'll find numbers, such as etched tally marks on walls, but on the whole you'll find paintings of hunting trips.[1] When ancient humans wanted to pass on knowledge, they shared stories of heroes for their kids to emulate.

Stories are memorable, exciting, and captivating. We love to hear tales of ordinary people who faced conflict, failed, picked themselves up, and found new strategies to overcome adversity. Stories make knowledge memorable and practical. They give us heroes to admire and feats to achieve.

The best educators are aligned with these aspects of human nature. Think back to your favorite teacher as a child. I'm willing to bet two things.

First, they made the subject come alive with captivating illustrations. Maybe they shared their own experience, talked about history or the news, or showed examples in class.

Second, they gave you the freedom to practice mimicking the people you learned about. You could take what they showed you, copy their behaviors, and apply their tactics yourself.

These teachers know how to create an environment where kids learn by doing what they do naturally.

Next time you have the chance, go watch kids play. They're almost always pretending to live out stories they've heard. They copy characters from their favorite shows, games, and books. Much of the time, they'll extend the story to include their friends, family members, and events from their own lives. In essence, they're applying what they learn from stories to the real world.

How to Use Story-Driven Learning

We would all learn much better if we copied kids. Find stories of successful people, and then practice using their tactics. This turns studying from a chore to a joy. It's the natural way we're meant to learn.

In essence, this is what author Polina Pompliano does with her newsletter, The Profile. She tells the amazing stories of unique people and draws out lessons from their lives that we can use for ourselves. As she told me once:

"

We would all learn much better if we copied kids. Find stories of successful people, and then practice using their tactics.

"

If I want to learn something new, whether it's about making better decisions or the French Revolution, I'll pick a person that best embodies the idea I want to learn about. I find that it's easier to have an emotional connection to a person, which then triggers my memory, and I actually learn and remember.[2]

I think that what's true of Polina is true of all of us. We learn best when we can connect an idea with a person and their story.

Consider an example. Let's say you want to learn about decision-making. You might think the best step is to go to school and study statistics. One of your first classes would introduce you to Bayes' Theorem, a famous formula for calculating probabilities. It goes like this:

$$P(A|B) = \frac{P(B|A) \cdot P(A)}{P(B)}$$

Let's be honest. Your eyes probably glazed over. Good luck remembering all those variables! Formula-first learning is difficult because formulas are boring. We don't naturally find them engaging. On the other hand, we're naturally drawn to interesting people.

So, what's a better way to learn?

Instead of beginning with Bayes' Theorem, you might start with the story of Annie Duke. She's one of the best female poker players in the history of the game.

How did she master her craft?

She used probability theories, like Bayes' Theorem, to make good decisions about how to make good bets.[3] The formula helped her figure out the likelihood of whether or not she could win based on the cards she saw on the table and how her opponents placed their bets. This strategy rocketed her to the top of the poker world. In 2010, she won the NBC National Heads-Up Poker Championship. Her lifetime earnings amount to millions of dollars.

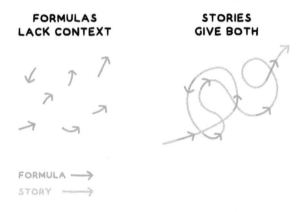

Now, all of a sudden, I bet you're much more interested in learning how to make decisions using statistics. You've wrapped all the numbers and theories around a person with a good story. Now that you've formed an emotional connection with a person, you're more likely to be interested in understanding their work.

I'm not saying mathematical formulas don't matter. Of course they do! If we want to master something, we need to know the technical details like the backs of our hands.

> We learn best when we can connect an idea with a person and their story.

However, to arrive at that ultimate goal, we need to begin in the right spot. We need to understand the why and how behind the formula—the story—before we can grasp the deeper meaning from the math. Stories help the learning fall into place.

You can use this same strategy for anything. If you want

to learn about engineering, you could read about the Wright brothers and then build a model plane. If you want to learn about fashion, you could start by reading about Coco Chanel and then design an outfit. If you want to learn about computers, read about Alan Kay and then program an app. If you want to learn about literature, read about Mary Shelley and then write a horror story. The examples are endless.

In the past, it was hard to learn from the stories of others. You'd have to read biographies of people from long ago or find a mentor in your local town. Now, that's all changed. The internet is overflowing with stories of amazing people from every area of life. Twitter, YouTube, Wikipedia, The Profile—everywhere you look, you can find someone to learn from.

> Stories make knowledge memorable and practical. They give us heroes to admire and feats to achieve.

Schools today are not leveraging the full potential of story-driven learning, but it's not entirely clear why. While story-driven learning is effective and fun, educators seem to prefer other less-effective techniques. For example, teachers rely too much on standard methods of rote memorization. Rather than making important information inspiring and memorable, they force kids through memory exercise after memory exercise, trying to meet the expected benchmarks with brute force.

But does this mean memorization is bad? Does it play a role in genuine learning? And if so, what's its place and how can we do it better?

Let's explore these questions by looking at...

8

*Learning
Through
Memorization*

TODAY, ANYTHING YOU want to know is a Google search away. Compared with the past, this changes how we should think about the role of memorization in education. Of course, memorization is still important, but for different reasons.

Instead of memorizing isolated facts, we need a strong foundation of general knowledge and a big box of thinking tools. We need mental models, cognitive skills, and the *why* behind how the world works. With information at our fingertips, we can afford to memorize less and analyze more.

In this chapter, we'll explore how memorization relates to genuine learning. We'll talk about the importance of pairing memorization with meaning, and unpack tactics that make memorization easier, more engaging, and longer lasting.

Pair Memory with Meaning

School gets things backward. In the words of Roger Lewin, "Too often we give our children answers to remember rather than problems to solve."

Kids learn to memorize things not to improve their understanding or critical thinking, but to score well on tests. They learn to parrot back the right answer—even when they don't know what it means.

As a teacher, I saw this dynamic when my students struggled to apply concepts they had memorized. As soon as they faced an open-ended question, they went blank. They could tell me the formula, but they didn't know how to put it into action.

Memorization makes it look like they're learning, but they're really imitating learning. They figure out how to give technically correct answers, even when they don't understand the concepts.

In reality, kids need to learn both the what and the why. They need to memorize important facts and learn what they mean. They need to know the reason things work the way they do.

For example, it's important for kids to memorize their multiplication tables. Otherwise, they're stuck with either their calculators or repeated mental addition, which are both inefficient. However, it's not enough to memorize that 3 x 5 = 15. They also need to understand that 3 x 5 = 15 means *three groups* with *five items* inside each group.

3 GROUPS OF 5
3x5=15

Genuine learning happens when we can get to the right answer because we understand how things work. It helps us store in our brains not only facts and figures but, more importantly, the reasoning process that leads us to these answers.

Focus on the Most Important Things

School tends to jump to memorization as the tool of choice. But it takes a lot of time and effort for knowledge to stick through pure memorization. Instead, teachers should only focus on the most useful information.

For example, is it the best use of a child's time to memorize the name and exact location of all 50 states? Yes, students should understand US geography in broad strokes. But will knowing the name and location of each state help them make important life decisions? Probably not.

Q DON'T MAKE KIDS

Q DON'T MAKE KIDS **MEMORIZE INFORMATION THEY CAN GOOGLE**

In general, we shouldn't force kids to memorize trivia in school. Trivia includes things that are:

- Not relevant to daily life.
- Not important for major decisions.
- Not fundamental to how the world works.
- Not hard to google.

The 50 states do not meet these criteria—but multiplication tables do, as suggested above. They're relevant to daily life, important for minor and major decisions alike, fundamental to how the world works, and not practical to google when we need to make a quick calculation. In short, we should focus less on memorizing trivia (like the 50 states) and more time mastering the ideas that matter most (like math).

For information worth remembering, however, good memorization tactics exist. That's what we will cover next.

Build a Memory Palace

Traditional forms of memorization are painful for both students and teachers. Flashcards and tears go hand in hand. Fortunately, there's a better way.

> Memorization makes it look like kids are learning, but they're really imitating learning.

The journalist Joshua Foer learned the *memory palace* method when he wrote a story about the US Memory Championships.[1] As he interviewed competitors, they insisted they weren't special. They said anyone could learn their techniques. So, Foer decided to practice the tactics himself—and went on to win the championship the next year.

In his book, *Moonwalking with Einstein*, Foer unpacks how memory competitors prepare.[2] The key is to recognize that our memories work exceptionally well. All we have to do is use them the way they're designed to work.

For example, we naturally remember two things quite well: places and unusual things. Numbers and facts, however, are boring. They just don't stick. So, to remember something bland, translate it into something memorable.

Think of a place dear to you, like your childhood home. Visualize it in your mind. Take a walk through all its rooms. Try to picture all the couches, chairs, and cabinets. Then take something hard to remember, like a grocery list:

- apples
- butter
- toilet paper

Put each item in a spot within your memory palace. The apples in the mailbox, the butter on the welcome mat, toilet paper on the kitchen counter.

In your mind, walk past the mailbox, through the front door, and into the kitchen. As you pass each item, picture it doing something ridiculous. Maybe the apples are singing, the butter is on fire, and the toilet paper is frozen. The crazier, the better.

Imagine what you would experience as you passed each item. You'd smile as you listened to the sweet song of the apples. You'd feel the heat radiating off the butter. A chill would run through your hand when you touched the toilet paper.

Now, when you go to the store, simply walk through your memory palace. Each item will automatically jump to mind. The place is so familiar to you, and the situation is so extreme, your memory won't have any problem telling you exactly what you need to remember.

With these tactics, we can turn memorization from a boring, frustrating task into an exciting activity that fuels lasting learning. All it takes is stepping back from how we traditionally try to remember facts and taking a tip from the professionals. When done right, memorization doesn't have to be hard. It can be fun and creative, fitting with the actual way our brains naturally work.

When used for the right purpose, memorization is a powerful tool for learning. It helps us retrieve information faster and store useful concepts in our minds.

But schools force kids to memorize things that aren't helpful for life (outside of scoring well on a test).

This misuse of the skill of memorization is one of the things that schools get wrong. This is part of a wider problem, where educators use methods that they've been told work wonders, but don't actually work well at all.

For example, many educators have fallen for...

Kids need a strong foundation of general knowledge and a big box of thinking tools. They need mental models, cognitive skills, and the why behind how the world works.

9

The Learning-Style Myth

YOU'VE PROBABLY HEARD that we each have a specific "learning style" that works best for us. In scientific jargon, this is called a *dominant sensory modality*. By the time we get to college, someone has told us that we are either "visual," "auditory," or "kinesthetic" learners and that we learn best in our preferred style.

But do people really have one specific learning style? And is it really best to customize learning to particular sensory modalities?

In this chapter, we'll challenge the concept of learning styles and examine whether there's a better way to think about the way people learn.

Learning Styles in My Classroom

According to the American Psychological Association, more than 90% of teachers believe students learn better if taught in their dominant learning style.[1]

I was one of those teachers.

I spent tons of time and effort trying to identify the learning styles of my students. I used a version of the VARK questionnaire (a tool for sorting kids by their learning preferences) to put my students into different buckets. Visual, auditory, kinesthetic.[2] I created different learning experiences for every group, tailoring my instruction to each student's learning style.

This took a lot of work, but "It's worth it," I thought. "Anything to help them learn."

I was wrong.

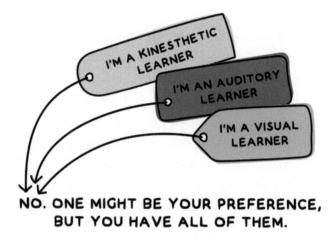

NO. ONE MIGHT BE YOUR PREFERENCE, BUT YOU HAVE ALL OF THEM.

While the idea of learning styles sounds logical and appealing, a number of studies now call this theory into question.[3]

Let's look at three important ways in which the idea of learning styles misses the mark.

The Problem with Learning Styles

First, we don't have one learning style. The idea that we have a dominant sensory modality is false. Visual, auditory, and motor input modalities in the brain are *interconnected*, and this interconnectedness is what helps us process information.

In other words, when we are learning, we engage more than one sense at a time.[4] For example, we may best learn how to cook by watching a YouTube video, but this does not mean we are visual learners. By learning to cook through a YouTube video, we are actually engaging sight, sound, and touch.

Second, tailoring instruction to various learning styles doesn't improve learning outcomes. It doesn't help students when we cater to their supposed learning style. In one study, for example, hundreds of students took the VARK questionnaire to determine their learning style.[5] The survey then asked them to prepare on a topic, using strategies that were supposed to match their learning style. The study found that: a) most students did not prepare in ways that seemed to reflect their learning style; and b) the few who did, didn't do any better on their assessment.

Third, learning styles encourage a fixed mindset. There is no benefit from categorizing people as visual, verbal, or kinesthetic learners. When we label or classify kids according to a learning style, we're encouraging a fixed mindset.[6] We're limiting them with self-fulfilling prophecies, despite our good intentions.

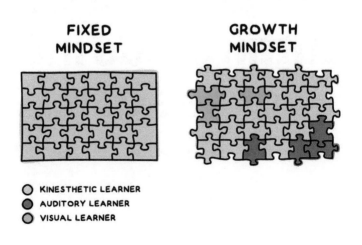

FIXED MINDSET   GROWTH MINDSET

○ KINESTHETIC LEARNER
● AUDITORY LEARNER
○ VISUAL LEARNER

"

Sometimes by celebrating kids' individuality we swing the pendulum too far and end up putting kids into boxes again.

"

Sometimes by celebrating kids' individuality—trying to find a learning style that is right for each person—we swing the pendulum too far and end up putting kids into boxes again.

When I was a teacher, I blindly adopted the idea of learning styles and fell prey to a popular myth about the brain and how it functions. Once I realized my mistake, I started rethinking learning styles and designing new ways to approach learning in my classroom.

Here are four tactics I started using with my students.

Tips for Better Action

First, clarify for kids that they don't have one learning style. They may have learning *preferences* or *predispositions* to process information a certain way, but we all learn best when we use a combination of many sensory modalities.

Second, emphasize that our learning preferences are not fixed. Our learning habits change over time and often depend on the situation. One day, we may prefer to learn about history by watching a documentary. The next day, we may want to read a blog post instead. This variety is good!

The idea that we have a dominant sensory modality is false.

Third, remind kids that they have a big toolbox of ways to learn. When they want to learn something new, encourage them to ask themselves, "Which mental tool (or tools) would work best for me on this topic and in this scenario?" The more kids realize the options available to them, the more prepared they'll be to teach themselves anything they want at any time, in any place.

Fourth, give kids opportunities to engage in many sensory

modalities. In this day and age, we have countless ways to learn: YouTube, books, podcasts, documentaries, online courses, bootcamps, online articles, and in-person study groups, to name a few. Let kids choose a topic and learn about it in three different ways. Help them reflect on what they notice.

> We all learn best when we use a combination of many sensory modalities.

Originally, teaching to a student's learning style was intended to make learning easier. As we've seen, teaching this way doesn't work, but at least the motivation behind it seems right. Or does it?

Is making learning easier for kids always best? Or will they become better learners if given the chance to struggle?

Let's talk about how...

10

*Confusion
Sparks
Curiosity*

H OW OFTEN DO you allow your kids to dwell on their confusion?

My guess is not much. We tend to see confusion as counterproductive to learning. But research tells us otherwise. Confusion is a powerful feeling. With the right approach, it can spark curiosity, which leads to motivation, engagement, and yes, learning.

In this chapter, we'll explore the benefits of embracing confusion. How can we help kids embrace their confusion and use it to their advantage?

Embracing Confusion

Consider this research study led by Professor Sidney D'Mello.[1] He and his colleagues discovered that confusion can increase learning and problem-solving. D'Mello summarized their findings this way:

> [We] find that confusion can be beneficial to learning if appropriately regulated because it can cause learners to process the material more deeply in order to resolve their confusion.[2]

This doesn't mean that all confusion in any amount is a positive thing. Not enough confusion and we get bored and tune out. Too much and we get frustrated and quit. Just right and we become curious and learn.

When we're confused, we're experiencing something psychologist Jean Piaget calls *cognitive disequilibrium*.[3] We're faced with new information that doesn't fit with our existing mental models. This drives us to dig deeper and move beyond our existing knowledge to gain a fuller understanding of how things work.

An example is learning division when we only know addition and subtraction. This new way of using numbers doesn't immediately connect with what we know about math. It challenges us to expand how we look at the world and adds new perspective to our mental toolbox. Or consider what it feels like to learn a new skill, such as programming, or how to play a challenging new video game. In all of these cases, cognitive disequilibrium is critically important for growth.

We can either avoid these moments of cognitive disequilibrium or seek them out and embrace them. We often try to avoid them because they're uncomfortable, demand lots of effort, and put us at risk of getting penalized when we're wrong.

But when we embrace these moments, disequilibrium can spark curiosity and push us to look for new answers.

Learning through Connections

It's really hard to embrace disequilibrium when new ideas are presented in isolation. This explains why students experience boredom and frustration in school. When we teach kids a subject like math alone and out of context, it's hard for them to see how the pieces fit together. This can make math seem incomprehensible and pointless.

Let kids engage in productive struggle and give them the chance to sort through their confusion.

Real learning comes from understanding the relationships and interactions across different disciplines. If we were to teach math as an exploration of relationships, with guidance toward noticing patterns, the process would be creative and highlight its utility and relevance.

At first, this change in how we teach subjects might sound too difficult. How will teachers find the time? Fortunately, small tweaks can make all the difference.

One way is using examples from the real world that kids are already curious about. If your child is interested in buying something, this is the time to teach them about money and counting. When they are interested in counting bigger numbers, you introduce them to a calculator. Maybe their interest in space and *Star Wars* fuels their interest in space time travel. Or if they're interested in dinosaurs they will probably want to learn about decades, centuries, and millennia... You get the idea. Learning through connections is entertaining and feels natural.

A Case Study: Synthesis

The goal of teaching should be to help kids change their perspectives so that they see difficult problems as exciting opportunities.

Think about how a builder like Elon Musk responds to tough problems. Others might drown in all the details of car production, solar energy, and space travel, but Elon gets excited by the challenge. He has a unique ability to handle complexity, and it isn't simply because of his intelligence. As much as his IQ, it is Elon's *mindset* that gives him such an advantage. He responds to confusion with curiosity.

Elon saw the value of this mindset and wanted to build a school that taught it to children. So, he hired his kids' school teacher, Josh Dahn, to design a new approach to education on the SpaceX campus. The result was a school called Ad Astra.[4]

The most popular class at Ad Astra was Synthesis. The idea behind it was simple—and brilliant: if we want to help kids solve tough problems, let them practice.

Josh designed a series of complex team games. Students competed to design the best SuperCharger network for Tesla and the best moonshot investments to move the American economy forward.

Synthesis became one of the students' favorite pastimes. They were confused and they *loved* it.

The simulations were constantly changing with new rules, new scoring variables, and new goals. Synthesis pushed kids into challenges without any directions or instructions, encouraging them to figure things out for themselves. It was a chance for kids to embrace chaos, explore crazy ideas, and come up with solutions no one else had thought of.

> Real learning comes from understanding the relationships and interactions across different disciplines.

Synthesis works because of the unique way it helps kids approach confusion. Let's look at three of its principles, which anyone can use.

Three Principles for Exploring Confusion

First, expose kids to confusion. Encourage kids to solve that harder math problem or read that challenging book. Let them explore complex ideas and help them understand that when they do, they are going to feel confused—and that's okay. When they play a new game, resist the urge to tell them the rules. Give them the chance to figure it out for themselves. Over time, you will notice they will start to enjoy it.

Second, up-end the way you talk about confusion with kids. Make sure they understand that confusion is not synonymous with failure or incompetence. Highlight the importance and

"

Give kids chance to embrace chaos, explore crazy ideas, and come up with solutions no one else had thought of.

"

relevance of confusion in the learning journey and respond to confusing moments with excitement and curiosity.

Third, don't jump to the rescue when kids get confused. We think we are helping them by making things easy and painless, but in reality, we are doing the opposite. Let kids engage in productive struggle and give them the chance to sort through their confusion. Be there to support them, but resist the temptation to jump in.

Exposure to a healthy amount of confusion offers significant benefits. The more kids experience confusion in the right context, the more they will be willing to wade through the feeling of not knowing—a key survival skill in today's world.

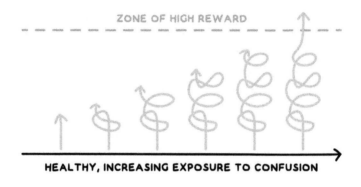

ZONE OF HIGH REWARD

HEALTHY, INCREASING EXPOSURE TO CONFUSION

By allowing kids to experience confusion, we're letting them get a taste of the real world. We're giving them the opportunity to learn how to handle complexity while the stakes are low so that later, they're mentally prepared when it matters. We're not letting them skate by with easy work, which feels good in the moment but hurts over the long term.

The truth is that *we* get uncomfortable when we watch kids

struggle through confusion, forgetting that in most cases they actually enjoy it.

Just watch them play one of their favorite video games. Most of the fun comes from figuring out how to solve a problem when it doesn't seem to make sense. In fact, once they've figured everything out, they usually stop playing and move on. A moderate amount of confusion is key to getting kids engaged.

What if we could take a page out of the game-design book? What if we could design learning experiences with engaging challenges that keep kids coming back for more?

In the next section, we'll answer these questions by exploring…

The
Power of
Games

11

The Architecture of Great Games

ONCE HAD a parent tell me that she was concerned her ten-year-old son had a retention problem. When I asked her why, she replied he wouldn't recall the names of the US state capitals, or the different parts of a cell.

I was surprised that she had jumped to this conclusion. After all, this kid knew every single Pokémon card out there.

The problem wasn't his memory. The problem was that he was just not interested in learning about the US capitals. When we asked him about it, he told us, "I'd rather learn the provinces of Panama, the place where I actually live."

My student had a valid point!

I saw this dynamic over and over again across grades: kids lack interest in things they don't find useful.

So, how can we reignite kids' interest in learning?

Mathematician and educator Seymour Papert points us in the right direction:

> Every maker of video games knows something that the makers of curriculum don't seem to understand. You'll never see a video game being advertised as being easy. Kids who do not like school will tell you it's not because it's too hard. It's because it's boring.[1]

We have a lot to learn from game designers. They sure know how to keep kids engaged. The experiences they create captivate kids and propel them to keep trying, even in the face of failure.

In this chapter, we'll look at three principles from video games that parents and educators can use to design compelling learning experiences: flow, intrinsically interesting challenges, and the Super Mario Effect. We will also examine the benefits of gaming.

Engagement
and Video Games

Why are games so captivating?

Renowned video game designer, Professor Jane McGonigal says it's because they put us in that "perfect state between feeling bored and feeling overwhelmed."[2] She goes on:

> You are always playing on the very edge of your skill level, always on the brink of falling off. When you do fall off, you feel the urge to climb back on.[3]

In other words, games put us into a psychological state called *flow*.

Flow was discovered by psychologist Mihály Csíkszentmihályi. He grew up in Europe during World War II and was struck by how many adults struggled to live a normal, satisfying life after the trauma they experienced during the war.[4] As a result, he decided to study what contributes to a life worth living.

Csíkszentmihályi pioneered a new kind of research called the Experience Sampling Method.[5] He asked people to record their activities, emotions, and other metrics at random intervals throughout the day. Through extensive study of this data, Csíkszentmihályi found that people described the same experience when at the height of enjoyment.

Csíkszentmihályi called this state flow.

In flow, we're entirely absorbed in a single task. We're totally aware of the present and feel in complete control. Time melts away.

Game designers work hard to develop experiences conducive to flow.[6] It's the main reason why games are so rewarding. They make it easy for players to feel *in the zone*.

To go into flow, you need three things:

1. **Clear goals:** you have a well-defined objective.
2. **Unambiguous feedback:** you can figure out how to improve with trial and error.
3. **A Goldilocks challenge:** your tasks are not too easy and not too hard.[7]

Most importantly, flow turns games into *intrinsically* rewarding experiences. People seek flow because they enjoy it—not because they might earn trophies or other rewards.

UNAMBIGUOUS   CLEAR   NOT TOO EASY,
FEEDBACK   GOAL   NOT TOO HARD

> **We have a lot to learn from game designers. The experiences they create captivate kids and propel them to keep trying, even in the face of failure.**

Game designers use these tactics to focus all of the player's attention on the game. We may think focus has more to do with raw willpower, but game designers win our focus by crafting *context* that draws our brains into flow.

Kids learn complicated skills in video games like critical thinking, problem-solving, resilience, strategy, and collaboration, to name a few. Why, then, do so many of them struggle to learn in class? Unlike games, classrooms aren't designed for flow:

- Goals aren't obvious to kids, even with great lesson plans.
- Feedback is ambiguous; they see displeased teachers, but they're not sure *why*.
- Challenges are not customized; they're too easy for some kids and too hard for others.

Sadly, a new trend has made things worse. You may recall teachers giving out points and prizes to *good* students for completing tasks or doing well on classroom activities. While these systems check some boxes by adding a few cosmetic elements of games to school work, they entirely miss the spirit of what makes true games so engaging.

Gamification or Pointsification?

Teachers all over the world try to apply gamification in their classrooms. See the student leaderboard on the wall, or the stickers collected on the corners of desks. We trade good behavior for pizza parties and study time for games of *Jeopardy!*

And not just teachers—parents try these techniques at home too.

I remember my mom tried to use a sticker system to get me to clean my room and do homework. And it worked! For about a week.

Even companies like Amazon try to gamify things to make work more exciting for employees. As one journalist reports, Amazon employees' "physical actions, assembling orders and moving items, are translated into virtual in-game moves. So, the faster someone picks items and places them in a box, for example, the faster their car will move around a virtual track."[8] The idea was to make the hard, boring labor in the Amazon facilities more interesting for workers.

Kids need meaningful challenges connected to their interests, not a way to earn meaningless rewards.

But these tactics aren't games. We can't merely add a ranking system and expect students to enjoy learning more. Kids need meaningful challenges connected to their interests, not a way to earn meaningless rewards.

In short, people call these tactics gamification, but they're really *pointsification*.[9]

Pointsification ties to external motivation—free time, tasty treats, or bragging rights. It's taking the things that are least essential to games like points, badges, and leaderboards, and making them the core of the experience.

The problem isn't that pointsification doesn't work. The problem is that it's not sustainable.

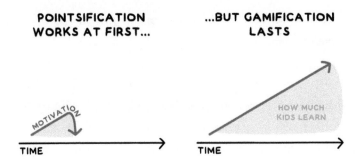

While pointsification may help tweak some behaviors in the short term, it doesn't work long enough to build actual skills and knowledge. This is because it teaches kids to love the rewards, instead of guiding them to cultivate a love for learning itself.

Pointsification misses the heart of what makes gaming effective for learning.

True gamification works much differently.

Games at the New York Public Library

In a true game, the player isn't only motivated by a future prize or reward. The player chooses to play out of genuine interest. If you stripped away the points and prizes, the game would still be attractive. McGonigal describes the goal of great game design this way:

What is that perfect state of challenge that brings out the best in us, so we're fully focusing our attention, feeling optimistic that we can succeed, but also curious because we're not sure and we feel like there's room for growth and personal development.[10]

I love the example that McGonigal shared on Patrick O'Shaughnessy's podcast.[11] The New York Public Library asked her for help with a specific problem: young people did not come to physical libraries anymore. The library had tried to solve this by offering points for checking out books and badges for visiting branches. But that is pointsification—which may work, but only for so long.

Why?

Because awarding points and badges didn't tap into what *intrinsically* could attract a young audience. Sure, some people would participate. But how many would form a meaningful relationship with the library just because they got points for checking out a book?

As McGonigal put it:

We need to figure out what feels like a real challenge to young people, and then give them that opportunity.[12]

McGonigal came up with a solution based on her approach to true gamification. Through research, she found that 92% of Americans under the age of 30 would want to write a book someday.[13] So, she proposed that the library design a game that would turn young people into published authors.

The game consisted of an overnight challenge in one of the library's underground floors with restricted access. The library invited guests over, outside of its usual working hours, and guided them to an underground room that is closed to the general public. They were then locked in the room!

Before being allowed to leave, each participant had to write a book. It was an intense, extreme challenge, but participants were so excited that they spent countless hours in the library. The game offered a meaningful reward that was worth the challenge. Participants were genuinely drawn to spending time at the library and developed a newfound appreciation for the place.

That's true gamification. Players came away feeling they had truly accomplished something *they* wanted. The reward of the game tied into something these people truly desired.

The trick to creating a true game is figuring out what your audience is interested in and tapping into those genuine challenges or desires. It's about coming up with a challenge that's so immersive it puts players in a flow state.[14]

Well-designed games produce more engagement, more excitement, and more fulfilling learning. These benefits alone are pretty great, but here is what is even more amazing: great games engage and excite us *even when we fail*. Players keep playing challenging levels over and over again even in the face of repeated defeat. Let's explore why.

The Super Mario Effect

No one likes to fail. But when it comes to video games, kids can spend most of their time failing and still *love* playing.

What is it about video games that keeps them optimistic in the face of failure?

Mark Rober, a former NASA and Apple engineer and current science YouTuber, ran an experiment to try to answer why kids can repeatedly fail at a game and yet keep playing.[15]

He had 50,000 participants attempt to solve a computer

programming puzzle. He assigned two different versions of the challenge.

In one version, if participants weren't successful, they got a message that said: "That didn't work. *Please try again.*" They did not lose points for failing.

In the other version, if participants weren't successful, they got a message that said: "That didn't work. *You lost 5 points. You now have 195 points. Please try again.*"

For those who lost points for failed attempts, their success rate in completing the puzzle was around 52%.

For those who did not lose points for failed attempts, their success rate was 68%. Participants in this group had nearly 2.5 times more attempts to solve the puzzle. On average, they learned more from trial and error and got better results.

My takeaway from Rober's experiment is that when mistakes are not penalized, people are more likely to keep trying. And if they keep trying, they have more chances of eventually succeeding.

> When mistakes are not penalized, kids are more likely to keep trying. And if they keep trying, they have more chances of eventually succeeding.

This sounds straightforward, yet in school we don't operate this way. Kids in school are taught that if they try and fail, they will get penalized with a bad grade that will go on their permanent record.

What if we reframed the learning process so that kids didn't worry about failure? How much more could they learn? How much more successful could they become?

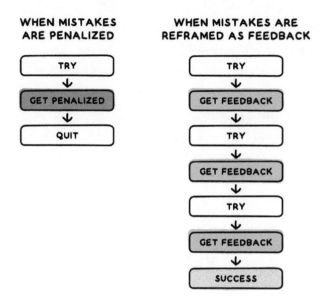

Mark Rober calls this the Super Mario Effect: focusing on the princess (the end goal) and not the pits (mistakes and failures), to stick with a task and learn more.[16]

In Super Mario, what matters is getting to the finish line and beating the game, regardless of how many tries it takes. Mistakes are seen as part of the learning process. Kids know that every time they fail, they gain insight into what they need to do next. Through trial and error, kids get really good and learn a ton in a very short amount of time.

When we frame learning challenges using the Super Mario Effect, kids actually want to keep learning. It feels natural to ignore the failures, get up, and try again.

We need to normalize making mistakes and learning from them. After all, most of the people, products, and ideas we admire today failed painfully on their way to success. Author J. K. Rowling was rejected 12 times before she found a publisher for *Harry Potter*.[17] Inventor James Dyson created 5,216 versions before he finally released his famous Dyson vacuum cleaner.[18] The lesson is clear: instead of making grades the priority, let's push kids to pursue their end goals, regardless of how many tries it takes them to get there.

Games can help us do this. They can help us shift kids from focusing on short-term marks or grades to focusing more on their ultimate end goals.

The Benefits of Video Games

Over 70% of kids play video games every day.[19] Of course, this striking statistic might be a sign of something very bad. Perhaps kids are getting addicted?

In the next chapter, we will examine that question more closely, but in the meantime, let's give kids the benefit of the doubt. Perhaps they enjoy video games for a good reason. What might that be?

According to physicist David Deutsch, video games help kids learn *how* to think. Other things might teach kids some content or a particular skill, but video games teach something more valuable: how to interact with the world.

Video games are essentially **simulations**. They give kids a chance to practice solving complex problems that mirror real life. The thinking skills they need to win games set them up for success as adults.

For example, video games helped entrepreneur Tobi Lütke build Shopify. Games like *Starcraft* taught him how to develop strategies, manage resources, and invest for the long term. These lessons directly transferred to his role as a CEO.

But the benefits of learning through games go beyond any specific lesson. Their real value is teaching kids how to teach themselves.

In Deutsch's words, with video games "you learn the mental skills with which you are learning the video game, and those skills are good for learning anything."

For this reason, Deutsch says that video games are destined to be an important means of human learning for the rest of history.

> Create an environment where kids keep iterating so they have plenty of chances to make progress.

They give us something that humanity has never had before, namely, "an interactive complex entity that is accessible at low cost and zero risk."

That's a big idea. Let's unpack it.

1. Complex

You can learn almost anything from a video game. They're a way to store and transfer human knowledge, just like books. Both books and video games are complex, but video games are also interactive.

2. Interactive

You can't practice with a book, but you can with a video game. You get to learn from taking action, making mistakes, and course correcting. In this way, video games are like learning the piano, but better.

3. Zero Risk

The piano is interactive but takes lots of time to learn—and few people go pro. It's risky. Video games are like conversations. You can dive in, learn, and not worry about losing a big investment. But for kids, conversations come at a cost.

4. Low Cost

Kids are afraid of looking stupid or getting in trouble when they talk to adults. It shouldn't be this way, but that's something they take away from school. Video games have nearly zero costs. You can make many mistakes, learn from trial and error, and keep playing.

Maybe we should rethink how we structure learning to mirror games. Parents do not struggle to get their kids to improve their skills playing *Mario Kart*, *Minecraft*, or *Roblox*. What if we designed education in the same way?

Practical Tips for Designing Learning Games

With a little creativity, we can make learning look a lot like a game. Let's explore five actionable principles for transforming education from work to play.

First, set up a goal centered around the players' authentic interests. McGonigal puts it this way: "You're looking for the challenge that's going to really bring the best out in people and really, when they achieve it, they feel like it was a meaningful and epic achievement." For example, few kids want to practice their handwriting with a worksheet, but many would love to write a story!

Second, pick an unnecessary obstacle for kids to voluntarily tackle. In many ways, this is what makes the difference between work and play. Are we forcing them to do something? Or is it a fun activity that they get to choose? Think about it this way: which of the following writing prompts sound more like a game?

- "Finish your story by noon or you'll lose iPad time!"
- "Let's see who can write the craziest story about grandma and turtles!"

Both scenarios focus on helping kids practice their writing, but the second is likely to work much better. The task is framed as a chance to play a game, not coercing kids into doing work.

Third, select the right level of difficulty. For the creative writing challenge, you could adjust the required length, number of characters, or the difficulty of the vocabulary words. You want to design the game so that it's neither too easy nor too hard. You don't want them bored or frustrated. You want them focused, excited, and a little puzzled.

Fourth, create a reliable feedback system for them to learn from failure. This system could be very simple. You could have them read their story to you and then share your thoughts. Sometimes, the most effective way to offer feedback is to ask them a question: "What do you think would make your story better?" Kids are often their own best critics. Most importantly, make sure they do not experience some type of neglect when their story doesn't meet your standards. Even a little bit of shame will sour the experience, discouraging them from trying again. The point is to create an environment where kids keep iterating so they have plenty of chances to make progress.

Fifth, set an authentic reward. As we've discussed, rewards can hurt flow if they're not designed carefully. Let's say you pick the reward of an extra 20 minutes of iPad time if your child writes a good story. In this case, the story and the reward are disconnected. As a result, they'll struggle to really learn because they're distracted by something else. However, let's say they're writing a story about grandma. In that case, a good reward would be a special trip to see grandma and read her their story. This incentive encourages deep engagement in the project rather than distracting from it.

> What if we reframed the learning process so that kids didn't worry about failure?

With these five principles, we can flip learning on its head. Instead of creating boring or frustrating tasks for kids, we can create genuine games that connect to their interests, encourage them to dive deep, tackle real challenges, learn from trial and error, and feel authentic satisfaction from their efforts.

Game design offers an incredible opportunity for parents and educators. It gives them tools to create engaging experiences that connect with kids' true interests and encourage them to keep pressing forward in the face of failure.

But games can also have a dark side. Can they become addictive? Don't they often encourage aggressive behavior? What if kids love them so much that they stop engaging in the real world?

Let's examine...

12

The Psychology of Healthy Gaming

KIDS SPEND AN average of 7.5 hours per day in front of screens.[1] They're watching videos, scrolling through social media, diving into online chat rooms, playing games, and so much more.

Why are these activities so attractive? Are they dangerously addictive, or do kids simply lack self-control?

In this chapter, we will explore why kids love screen time. We'll also discuss the deep psychological factors at play and talk about how to help children develop a healthy relationship with technology. Finally, we'll talk about video games in particular and how to encourage kids to enjoy the benefits while avoiding the pitfalls.

But first, we need to answer an important question. What motivates us? What drives us to do anything at all?

Motivation and Self-Determination

Self-determination theory says that humans are motivated by three things:

1. **Autonomy**: making our own choices.
2. **Competency**: building skills and knowledge.
3. **Relatedness**: connecting with like-minded peers.[2]

We crave these experiences just like our bodies crave protein, carbs, and fats. If we don't eat right, our bodies break down. In the same way, if we don't feed our psyches with autonomy, competency, and relatedness, our mental health suffers.

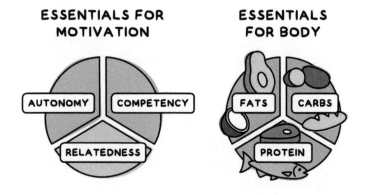

Unfortunately, many kids don't get enough of these essential experiences. As author Nir Eyal says in his book *Indistractable*:

School, where kids spend most of their waking hours, is in many ways the antithesis of a place where kids feel competence, autonomy, and relatedness.[3]

This problem raises an interesting question. Are kids searching for supplements online because they can't find autonomy, competency, and relatedness in their offline world?

Let's unpack this idea by looking at the daily life of a kid in school and comparing this to time kids spend online.

Motivation During Daily School Life Versus Online

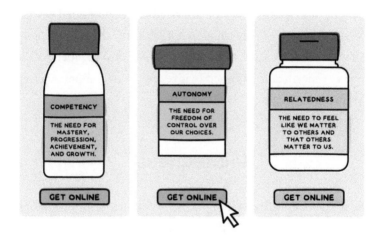

Autonomy

In school, most everything is planned with strict rules. Kids are told what to do, what to think, and even what to wear! One survey found that the average kid has to follow twice as many restrictions as an incarcerated felon (crazy, I know!).[4]

By contrast, kids have tons of autonomy online. They can make choices (like what and who to play with), dive deep into what interests them, and make decisions of their own (such as what their avatar should look like). They experience a lot less adult control and surveillance.

Competency

Kids are so different. We can't expect them all to learn the same way or force them into one box. The recent obsession with metrics, standards, and one-size-fits-all curriculums makes it hard for kids to experience competency in school.

On the internet, kids can learn anything they want! They get to teach themselves new subjects, which gives them confidence in their abilities to learn on their own. Many turn to video games, which are specifically designed to give a sense of competence and achievement.

Relatedness

One of the main reasons why parents send their kids to school is so they can make friends and develop social skills. Unfortunately, kids don't have as much time to socialize as they used to in schools. Packed schedules and extensive curriculums leave little room for them to play and connect.

On the other hand, the internet is perfect for finding like-minded people. It's like a big playground, where people can connect over their shared interests. Kids can build friendships through free play, spending hours together diving into games and working on projects they choose.

No wonder kids spend so much time online! It provides them with the autonomy, competency, and relatedness that they so often lack in their daily lives.

But what about when screen time goes from an important outlet to an unhealthy obsession? Let's look at seven tactics for helping kids when their screen time starts to take over their lives.

Helping Kids Navigate Screen Time

First, discuss the pros and cons of screen time together. It's easy to fall into the trap of laying down rules without giving good reasons. That's a quick way to frustrate kids! Instead, start a conversation together about technology, its benefits, and its costs. The goal is for kids to learn how to cope with overuse on their own so that they do what's good for them when we're not around.

Second, show you understand their struggle. Say things like, "It must be hard to be told what to do all day. I bet it feels good to choose what you want to do when you play *Minecraft*." When kids feel understood, they are more receptive to our suggestions and can plan better ways to spend their time.

Third, acknowledge how you face similar challenges. Say things like, "I've noticed I waste a lot of time on my phone in the morning. When I wake up, I'm going to read a book instead." Model the proper use of technology. Vulnerability builds trust.

Fourth, address screen time in an autonomy-supported way. Don't make more rules that limit kids' autonomy. Instead, create boundaries for screen time together in a collaborative way. Make sure your interest in their online activity isn't purely negative.

Spend time with them online, take an interest in what they enjoy, and learn to value what they value before you encourage limits.

Fifth, provide opportunities for real-world fulfillment. Give kids the chance to enjoy agency, competency, and relatedness offline as well as online. Limit adult-led activities. Give them lots of free time, let them explore many hobbies, and organize plenty of playdates with friends.

Sixth, encourage more creation and less consumption. When your kids do spend time online, encourage them to learn, make, socialize, and create. The goal is fewer cat videos and more time learning to code; less time scrolling social media and more time creating content.

Seventh, offer a better "Yes." Make sure that when you do ask your kids to say "No" to their screens, they're saying "Yes" to something even better. Make family time so fulfilling and engaging, your kids won't miss their phones.

It's important for us to slow down before we get frustrated with how much time our kids spend in front of screens. What are their motivations? How might we find more healthy channels for them to enjoy the experiences they're craving? As Nir Eyal says:

> Knowing what's really driving their overuse of technology is the first step to helping kids build resilience instead of escaping discomfort through distraction. Once our kids feel understood, they can begin planning how best to spend their time.[5]

The average kid has to follow twice as many restrictions as an incarcerated felon.

The goal is to bring together kids' offline and online worlds in a healthy, fulfilling way.

Tactics for Healthy Gaming

But what about video games specifically?

For a long time, researchers and concerned parents worried about their dangerous effects.[6] Aren't they addictive for kids? What if they spend so much time playing games that they never learn how to interact with people in the real world? And what about first-person shooter games, where kids often spend hours killing human-looking characters? Do these encourage violent behavior?

Jane McGonigal conducted a meta-analysis of more than 500 research papers.[7] She wanted to understand what caused video games to be beneficial or harmful for young people. She proposes four tactics that parents can use with kids to encourage healthy gaming.

Are kids searching for supplements online because they can't find autonomy, competency, and relatedness in their offline world?

First, examine whether kids are playing with an escapist mindset or playing with purpose. McGonigal found that the key determinant is the question of *why* kids are playing the game in the first place. Are they playing to escape real life? Or are they playing to pursue a goal that matters to them?

Kids who play games to escape—that is, to block unpleasant emotions or avoid confronting stress—have a very difficult time translating their game skills to real life. This approach tends to increase depression, worsen social isolation, and, in cases, lead to addiction.

On the other hand, kids who play games with a purpose—that is, to spend quality time with friends and family, learn something new, or improve a skill—are able to activate their in-game strengths in real-world contexts.

Second, help kids keep their gaming under 21 hours per week. Games benefit us mentally and emotionally when we play up to three hours a day, or 21 hours a week. When we play more than 21 hours a week, the benefits of gaming start to decline and are replaced with negative impacts on our health, relationships, and real-life goals. So far, no study has found negative impacts on people (kids and adults) who play video games less than 21 hours a week.

Third, reverse the order: first play games, then study. If we want kids to retain what they study better, they should play video games first, then study before going to sleep. While it may sound counterintuitive, studies show that when we go to sleep, our brain focuses on the most salient problem it was recently trying to solve (think *The Queen's Gambit*). So reverse the order: first play, then study.

Fourth, encourage kids to avoid playing aggressive, competitive games against strangers online. Excessive competition against strangers online can have a negative social impact, particularly in games with strong themes of domination and destruction like *Call of Duty*. However, no research shows that *Call of Duty* increases hostility or aggression when played with people you know in real life.

The effect of video games is different if we are playing against someone we know rather than playing against a stranger—a stranger that we can sometimes dehumanize. A good rule of thumb is for kids to spend no more than half of their play time trying to beat strangers online. They are better off trying to beat their friends and family, or playing cooperatively with strangers.

When we're worried about our kids' screen time, we're tempted to jump into action and start enforcing hard and fast rules, but this approach can often compound the problem. We might accidentally be taking away kids' only chance to experience meaningful autonomy, relatedness, and competency.

Instead, we should take the time to understand *why* they're using their devices, *how* they're using them, and the specifics about what is and isn't healthy for their development. Most importantly, we need to involve kids in the process.

> Bring together kids' offline and online worlds in a healthy, fulfilling way.

We need to draw close to them, give them a voice, and study the pros and cons of technology together. We need to be part of the solution by setting a positive example of how they can experience autonomy, relatedness, and competency in the real world.

Encouraging our kids to lead a healthy relationship with technology and video games will spark in them more fulfillment and empowerment—two emotions that are critical for...

Raising Successful Kids

13

*Skin in
the Game*

N LIFE, OUR choices have consequences, both good and bad. We should be held responsible for those consequences. Otherwise, we are less likely to learn from our mistakes.

In other words, we need *skin in the game*.

Author Nassim Taleb describes skin in the game like this: those who make a decision should also shoulder its risks.[1] We shouldn't just be rewarded for our good results. We should also be accountable to handle the fallout when things go wrong. Without skin in the game, we don't have a reason to correct our errors.

In this chapter, we'll talk about why both kids and parents should put more skin in the game of education. Kids need more opportunities to make decisions and wrestle with the outcomes of their choices. Parents need to take more responsibility for their children's learning. When they do, both child and parent will experience more fulfillment, more engagement, and more learning.

Skin in the Game
for Kids

At a first glance, it might seem like school holds kids accountable. For example, kids who do poor work earn poor grades. It's true that report cards give kids some skin in the game—but it's a game they fundamentally don't buy into. It's skin in the game of school. And the game of school is much less relevant to them than the game of life.

Kids are hungry for the real thing. They don't want more worksheets and assignments. They want to solve problems that mirror the real world.

They want stakes that matter to them.

But letting kids tackle real problems also means allowing them to wrestle with the results of their decisions. After all, that's the hardest part of real-life choices: dealing with the consequences when things go wrong.

From a distance, this might sound scary, but skin in the game actually has three important benefits for learning.

First, skin in the game sets up the right conditions for real learning. When the stakes are high, our bodies direct all our energy to our brains. Our mental vision clears. Our thoughts focus. Our motivation kicks into gear.

> Kids are hungry for the real thing. They want stakes that matter to them.

Second, skin in the game makes learning more *memorable*. Our brains sear what we learn from hard experience into our neural networks. Those lessons stick with us for life!

Third, skin in the game makes learning more *exciting*. As Taleb says, he didn't care for statistics in school, but then he learned about options trading.[2] All of a sudden, his knowledge of probability meant the difference between making and losing millions of dollars!

Of course, the key to better education isn't putting kids in charge of large investment portfolios. We need ways for them to experience high-stakes scenarios that mirror reality without the possibility of life-changing failure.

That's what Josh Dahn created for Synthesis. As we saw in

chapter 10, Synthesis started as a series of complex challenges and conundrums for kids. For example, "If you could pay a teacher, a firefighter, a soldier, a police officer, or the mayor between $1 and $5, who would you pay the most and why?"

It's mind blowing to hear kids reason through these kinds of questions. They have to consider deeper dilemmas (How big is the town? Does the teacher care about the students? Does this police officer treat the community with respect?), assign value relative to everyone else, and back up their opinions with evidence.

Conundrums push kids to understand tradeoffs, forcing them to make decisions and judgments in a world where there are no right answers. They force kids to craft an explanation full of *nuance* and realize that the world they live in is not black and white.

> Kids want to solve problems that mirror the real world.

And while conundrums are great, Josh intuited that kids would learn more if they put skin in the game. So he turned the conundrums into competitive simulations.[3]

In Josh's original conundrums, learning rarely moved past conversation. But in his more advanced simulations, kids could practice implementing their ideas and responding to the downstream effects. There were real winners and losers. Competition creates real stakes!

For example, in the Synthesis game *Art for All*, kids bid against each other on different pieces of artwork. The goal is to curate a collection that people will buy tickets to see. If they bid too high, they'll waste money and won't turn a profit, but if they bid too low, the other teams will acquire all the best paintings. In this simulation, the students have to craft a strategy, think on their feet, and make quick decisions.

Most importantly, the Synthesis simulations give kids

problems that are fun to solve. Students get to run movie studios, colonize space, fish the oceans, and so much more. Kids learn because the problems are interesting and they're invested in the outcome.

Synthesis simulations give kids a unique opportunity: they get to practice solving real problems that mirror the real world with real stakes, without the threat of making mistakes with long-term consequences.

We need more opportunities like this for kids. They need the chance to practice not only making lifelike decisions, but also responding when things don't turn out like they expected.

After all, those are the hardest kinds of challenges they will face as adults. What do you do when your choices have unexpected consequences? We can't expect kids to be prepared for these kinds of problems in the real world if they haven't ever wrestled with them before.

Skin in the Game for Parents

Kids aren't the only ones who need more skin in the game. Parents need it too.

Most parents drop their kids off at school and hope for the best. But outsourcing all of our kids' education to the school system isn't a great idea. Skin in the game means digging into the work instead of delegating all of it to others. For parents, it may mean teaching your kids a little yourself rather than always relying only on schools and teachers.

Let's look at four specific reasons why putting skin in the game is so important for parents.

"

Getting involved in your kids' education allows you to make the most of the relatively short time you have to directly impact their future.

"

First, it gives kids more stability. In school, kids are constantly moved from class to class and from grade to grade. All of these changes can make kids feel unknown and misunderstood. But if their parents are deeply engaged in their education, then kids have a throughline. They have a consistent, caring voice in a parent who knows them and understands their strengths and weaknesses, talents, and areas for growth.

Second, it gives parents more insights. No standardized test or expert opinion can compare to the knowledge that you will gain by teaching your kid yourself. As a result, skin in the game makes it much easier for you to make the hard but necessary choices required for them to excel in their education. You have the understanding you need to partner with your kids to make decisions that are personalized to them and designed to help them develop into well-prepared adults.

> Kids need more opportunities to make decisions and wrestle with the outcomes of their choices.

Third, it helps you fill gaps in their learning. Teachers are responsible for educating dozens of kids. The best teachers will try to adapt to each student, but they can only do so much. Inevitably, some students get left behind and others get held back. If you get yourself involved in your kid's education, however, you can offer your child a more tailored learning experience. You can focus more on their favorite subjects and provide extra help when they're struggling.

Fourth, it lets you maximize your time with your children while you can. Kids spend their most formative years with their parents. We have a unique opportunity to partner with them and prepare them for the rest of their lives. But the window to influence them during their early years will be over in a flash! Getting involved in your kids' education allows you to make the most of the relatively short time you have to directly impact their future.

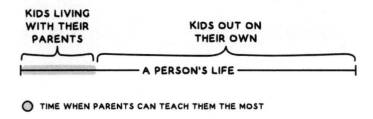

With those four reasons, we have looked at *why* supplementing kids' education at home is important. Now let's look at *how*.

How to Put More Skin in the Game

Teaching makes most parents nervous. Many are already busy with work and other family commitments, overwhelmed with packed schedules. Others lack confidence because they're not trained educators.

These are legitimate concerns. But in reality, you don't need an education degree or lots of free time to play a role in your kids' education.

You can choose from a spectrum of options. On the one end is homeschooling, where parents do all the teaching themselves. On the other end is traditional school, where parents mostly outsource the work to others.

SKIN IN THE GAME SPECTRUM

The goal is to move as much as possible from the left side of the spectrum to the right. But you don't need to go all the way to homeschooling. There's lots of room in the middle.

As you explore options in the middle, here are five things to consider.

First, learn the different educational options available for your kid. Take responsibility for making researched, intentional decisions. Experiment with different programs, methods, and alternative schools. See what works for *your* kid. Check out the section titled "How to Exit the System (without Leaving School)" at the end of this book for some recommendations.

Second, pick a topic your kid will learn at home. You can make this manageable by starting with one subject. You may pick something you loved as a kid, or something your child is eager to learn more about. Maybe it's history, literature, math, or programming. Only a couple of hours per week will make a huge difference. Even if you get some things wrong, you're engaged. That's what matters. If you don't have enough expertise on the subject, take this as an opportunity to learn about something new with your child. Be novices together!

Third, dive into a passion project with your kid. Maybe your kid loves baking, building, or coding websites. Pick something to do together that your kid is passionate about. If your kid wants to dance, come up with a choreography together. The key is to grow along with them, set a positive example, and keep it fun.

Fourth, let kids change their minds. Let's say you pick the best alternative school, subject, or passion project—but your kid hates it. Then move on! If you didn't like something, you'd quit. Give your kid the same opportunity. What matters is that you're involved in the process.

Fifth, don't blame teachers, schools, or tutors. It's tempting to offload responsibility when things go wrong, but don't fall into that trap. If things aren't working, face the challenge head-on and find new solutions. That's the core principle of skin in the game.

I wish I could say this is easy. It's not. But I can say that the effort is absolutely worth it. As with the rest of life, the most rewarding things are the hardest.

Keep in mind that skin in the game has two sides: your side and your child's side. Both are critically important for striking the right balance.

Kids benefit when their parents take some responsibility for their education, but kids benefit even more when they have some ownership over their learning. That means we need to practice the art of engaging with our kids without taking total control or overprotecting them.

That's the key to...

14

Raising Antifragile Kids

W E WANT TO make our kids feel safe and protected, but we sometimes overplay our hand.

As a result, we are dealing with a generation of children that are sensitive and risk-averse—children who seek adults to solve their problems and protect them from discomfort.[1]

But kids are not as fragile as we think.

In this chapter, we will look at the downsides of overprotective parenting. We'll talk about how our instinct to keep our kids from experiencing difficulties and stress can backfire, setting them up for failure later in life. Lastly, we'll discuss the benefits of exposing kids early to moderate levels of stress and reasonable risks.

Fragility in the Classroom

It's not easy to see a child suffer, so it's normal for adults to want to intervene when a child is upset. In some cases, however, when we feel like we're protecting our children, we really aren't.

Rejection, failure, pain, and discomfort are feelings that we experience throughout our lives. Going out of our way to protect children from these is rarely a good idea. The earlier they learn to

> Kids are not as fragile as we think. The earlier they learn to face and tolerate difficulties, the better prepared they will be for life.

face and tolerate difficulties, the better prepared they will be for the rest of their lives.

I experienced this dilemma in my classroom. I taught bright children who had difficulty handling small setbacks and suffered at the slightest bit of disappointment. I fought my desire to intervene. By facing challenges on their own, I reminded myself, children grow stronger into adulthood.

Children grow stronger from facing challenges, moderate pain, and low-stake conflicts.

I found that for some of my classroom parents, however, this wasn't as straightforward. One parent told me:

Ms. Fabrega, please help me convince my daughter to opt out of the talent show auditions this year. She insists on doing a solo dance, but she is not ready and I don't want to see her suffer.

Another one said:

I would appreciate it if my child is not present when you discuss the 9/11 incident, as she is sensitive and I'd prefer she doesn't find out about it.

These are just some (of many) examples of parents aiming to protect their children from minor setbacks. While done with the best intentions, these interventions could have unintended consequences. The line between these well-meaning actions and *overprotection* is thin.

Parents want their children to make their own decisions, think for themselves, and solve their own problems. But they are reluctant to give kids independence because they fear that something will go wrong. This harms children over the long term.

Overprotected children can't handle disappointments without adult intervention. Used to being helped, they get discouraged at the sight of a challenge. They suffer from low self-esteem, as they feel like they can't do anything by themselves. Overprotection makes children feel entitled and fragile.

We want our children to be the opposite of fragile—we want them to be *antifragile*.

The Power of Antifragility

A term coined by author Nassim Taleb, antifragility describes things that become stronger when exposed to stress and randomness.[2] Contrary to the fragile, which breaks when exposed to stress, the antifragile needs stress to thrive.

Children grow stronger from facing challenges, moderate pain, and low-stake conflicts. They do best when given the freedom to fail and navigate through the ups and downs of life.

> No matter how hard we try, we can't prevent every bad thing from happening to kids.

Children *are* antifragile.

It is our job to continue cultivating their antifragility by not intervening when they face moderate stress. Heck, we should push them toward it!

I did so in my classroom, and loved seeing how my students grew stronger. I observed from a distance before intervening in minor conflicts. When intervening, I let them do the talking first and taught them to reflect. I encouraged them to try and solve problems on their own before asking for my help. I made them take risks—"Of course you should try out for the basketball team!"—and face challenges.

No matter how hard we try, we can't prevent every bad thing from happening to kids. We don't have that much control over their lives. At times they will fail, and at times they will suffer. But as long as the failure and suffering are not chronic, they will grow stronger and thrive.

Let children experience discomfort and deal with difficult people. Let them take a few bruises, bumps, and scars in a relatively safe environment, like school or soccer practice.

Just like exposing kids early to germs will help them develop stronger immune systems, exposing them to difficult situations will help them become more resilient, independent, and self-confident.

Good parenting, like good teaching, is about mastering the art of balance. It's about keeping a close eye, but not intervening all that much; making children feel safe and protected, but not that much either. Doing nothing is often better than doing something.

Exposing kids to difficult situations will help them become more resilient, independent, and self-confident.

Although this is difficult at first for both children and parents, stronger, antifragile adults will thank us in the future.

The goal of raising antifragile kids isn't only to make them resilient, though that's certainly a big part of it. We want kids who can persevere through all the ups and downs of life. But we also want our kids to become mature, ethical adults. By letting them struggle, we give them a chance to build character.

> Good parenting, like good teaching, is about mastering the art of balance.

To see how, let's discuss...

15

How to Develop
Character Like
the Stoics

FOR THOUSANDS OF years, teachers had big goals for their students. They didn't simply want smart kids with strong memorization skills. They wanted their students to become good and wise people with strong character. Their aim was to create virtuous citizens prepared to lead society forward through its toughest times. Teachers relied on Stoicism as one of their most powerful tools.

Stoicism is a philosophy that started in Ancient Greece, where its followers were known as the Stoics. At first, it was a theoretical worldview about how nature works, but after a few hundred years, it turned into an exceptionally practical guide for life. Stoicism taught the importance of self-control, perseverance, and moral virtue for living a good life.

Throughout history, some of the world's greatest leaders studied Stoicism, from the Roman emperor Marcus Aurelius, to America's first president, George Washington. Even today, successful people across industries still use Stoicism, from President Bill Clinton to Secretary of Defense James Mattis, actress Anna Kendrick, football coach Nick Saban, and author J. K. Rowling.

When you hear about a leader today who discovered Stoicism, it was almost always through their own personal research. That's because it's rarely taught in modern school.

Perhaps "Stoicism" sounds old and irrelevant, "philosophy"

seems impractical, or the idea of "virtue" has fallen out of style. Whatever the reason, we should bring Stoicism back into education.

We need to revisit old Stoic teachings and make character development an essential part of the student learning experience.

In this chapter, we'll talk about the Stoic idea of virtue and its benefits for kids. We'll also unpack four practical techniques we can use today to help our kids develop strong moral character.

The Four Stoic Virtues

The first Stoic virtue is *courage*. Courage is the bravery to face adversity. It doesn't mean we're never scared, but that when we're scared, we decide to take action instead of running away. It's the will to press forward, put our butts on the line, and our skin in the game.

The second Stoic virtue is *temperance*. Courage is wonderful, but we go too far when we take unnecessary risks. It's a spectrum: cowardice on the far left, recklessness on the far right, and courage in the middle. We should be brave, not fearful, but we should also avoid foolishness. That's temperance.

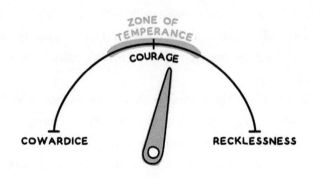

The third Stoic virtue is *justice*. For the Stoics, justice is the highest virtue. It means that we exist for the sake of others, not ourselves. Everything we do should contribute to the good of society. We must treat others the way we want to be treated and act with honesty, respect, and fairness.

The fourth Stoic virtue is *wisdom*. Wisdom means making our philosophy work in the real world. What's the right amount of courage? How do I act with justice in this situation? Wisdom helps us answer these questions, turn our ideas about virtue into action, and make choices with long-term benefits.

Courage, temperance, justice, and wisdom—four powerful principles for guiding our decisions. But how can we help kids make the leap from knowing these virtues in their heads to using them in their lives?

Here are four tactics that you and your kids can employ in everyday life.

Four Tactics for Using Stoicism Today

First, read stories of heroes to your kids. It's hard to grasp the benefits of virtue without concrete examples. That's what makes stories so powerful, especially classic ones from history.

Greek mythology was designed for this specific purpose. You tell them of Hercules, who chose a life of courage over pleasure and ease. Or Odysseus, who used wisdom to escape dangerous enemies like the Cyclops. With clear examples in mind, it's easier

> "We need to revisit old Stoic teachings and make character development an essential part of the student learning experience."

for kids to understand virtue, see its benefits, and integrate it into their lives.

Second, help them focus on what they can control. Talk with kids about how they can't always control what happens, but they can control how they respond. Sometimes, friends decide to be mean—but that doesn't mean we have to be mean back.

For example, instead of lashing out in anger, kids can practice calming down by reciting each letter of the alphabet silently to themselves. They can take a pause and practice temperance and justice.

Third, encourage them to use a virtue journal. Journaling is an important part of Stoicism, but the Stoics didn't keep ordinary journals. They didn't just write down the events of their day and their emotions. Instead, they kept track of their principles and focused on growing their character.

> Talk with kids about how they can't always control what happens, but they can control how they respond.

Ordinary journals help kids develop self-awareness, but a virtue journal adds an extra benefit: healthy self-criticism.

For example, they might journal about a tough interaction they had with a friend at school. What happened? How did they react? In what ways did they show courage or temperance? How could they respond better next time?

A virtue journal provides kids with an open space to reflect on areas of growth and improvement as they work to become better people.

MAKING SENSE IN YOUR HEAD IS HARD...   ## ...BUT EASIER WHEN YOU WRITE IT DOWN

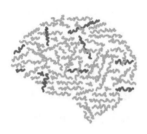

Fourth, talk about how virtue is like a muscle. Sometimes, kids might feel discouraged by the big gap between who they are and who they want to become. That's why it's so important to talk about how virtue is like a muscle.

Character building is essential for helping kids grow up into well-rounded adults.

When we first go to the gym, we want instant results, but to make progress, we have to show up consistently and put in the effort. It's the same with virtue. It's hard at first, but with enough time, effort, and reflection, our character grows stronger and stronger.

Character building is essential for helping kids grow up into well-rounded adults. It gives them a stable north star, guiding them through tough decisions, showing them how to treat others well, and providing them with stability throughout the storms of life.

This raises an important question. Besides character, what else do we want our kids to have as adults? We hope for them to grow into good, virtuous, moral people—but don't they need something else as well?

Let's transition from philosophy to practice.

How do we set up kids to make a unique contribution to the world?

We'll explore this in the next chapter by looking at...

16

Range &
Specific
Knowledge

F WE WANT exceptional kids, we should force them to specialize early... right?

It's time to bust this myth.

In this chapter, we'll discuss the relationship between range, generalization, specialization, and specific knowledge. We'll talk about how to help kids develop a broad base of knowledge, explore many different areas, and discover where they can add unique value to the world.

Let's start by looking at *range*.

Helping Kids Develop Range

In some fields, early specialization works well. Think about golf. Tiger Woods picked up his first putter at seven months old. At two, he was on TV hitting golf balls with Bob Hope. At four, he was practicing eight hours a day, winning bets against adults.[1]

Early specialization worked for Tiger because golf is a *predictable* sport. The skills he learned at two applied to golf for the rest of his life. It's a stable game. Very little changes.

But few things in life are like golf.

We live in a world filled with ambiguity and complexity. Today, the people who succeed the most know how to navigate constant change. They draw on a generalist background, which equips them to mix different approaches together to face new and unexpected challenges.

The people who succeed the most know how to navigate constant change.

In his book *Range*, David Epstein argues that "many of the most effective people in elite professional fields (such as sports, art, and scientific research) succeed not despite the fact but because they find their way to that particular field after pursuing other endeavors first."[2]

Consider, for example, Nobel-prize-winning scientists. At first, you might expect them to be a picture-perfect case of highly specialized thinkers—and they are. But they're also broadly educated generalists as well. As Epstein summarizes:

> Compared to other scientists, Nobel laureates are at least twenty-two times more likely to partake as an amateur actor, dancer, magician, or other type of performer. Nationally recognized scientists are much more likely than other scientists to be musicians, sculptors, painters, printmakers, woodworkers, mechanics, electronics tinkerers, glassblowers, poets, or writers, of both fiction and nonfiction.[3]

In other words, generalism and specialism are friends, not enemies. But the order matters. Generalize, *then* specialize. Not the other way around!

Why?

When kids specialize early, it's easy for them to fall into "functional fixedness," a narrow mindset where they only see things one way.[4] They may miss creative solutions because they only ever mastered a single set of skills.

On the other hand, early generalism gives kids a firm

foundation of broad knowledge. Their eyes are open to many different perspectives. They have a big box of thinking tools, which helps them innovate in their specialty later in life.

LET THEM ENGAGE IN MANY THINGS...   **...SO THEY KNOW WHAT TO DOUBLE DOWN ON**

So, before you sign up your eight-year-old for daily golf lessons, try these tactics to help them develop range.

First, encourage a sampling period for new activities and interests. This will provide kids with the opportunity to try different sports, arts, or instruments without any pressure to commit.

Second, let kids engage in unstructured play. Unstructured play is play that isn't organized or directed by an adult and that doesn't have a pre-defined purpose or outcome. Encourage them to engage in imaginative play, create art or music, build forts out of random materials, and come up with stories with crazy twists and role-play them. This kind of play gives kids a sense of autonomy and the freedom to find new interests. It also allows them to learn more about themselves and make mistakes without worrying about failure. To help kids get the most out of unstructured play, make sure they have access to different materials, a big space, and plenty of time. Keep in mind that initial boredom is part of the process.

Third, facilitate self-reflection. After kids try new things, prompt them to reflect on their experience by asking questions like:

- "How did that feel? What felt really good?"
- "What surprised you the most?"
- "What was challenging?"
- "What do you think will work better next time?"
- "How long do you think it takes people to get good at this?"
- "Was there anything that you thought was going to be challenging or scary that ended up being the opposite?"
- "What do you think you would get better at with time if you kept coming back?"

These types of questions will help them grow to better understand themselves and their innate talents and passions.

Fourth, expose kids to a diverse learning diet. Expose them to various subjects and different types of thinking through books, movies, museums, sports, music, cultures, friend groups, religions, and philosophies.

As you can see, range is not about forcing your kids to get As in every subject or enrolling them in five different after-school programs at the same time.

Instead, it's about letting them explore, play, and try many different things. It's about cheering them on when they venture outside their comfort zone. Above all, it's about celebrating with them as they discover what they love to do most. In other words, range is about helping kids discover their *specific knowledge*.

Discovering Specific Knowledge

Specific knowledge is what you—and *only you*—can offer the world. Entrepreneur and investor Naval Ravikant describes it as "this weird combination of unique traits from your DNA, your unique upbringing, and your response to it. It's almost baked into your personality and your identity. Then you can hone it."[5]

The following table provides examples of what different people's specific knowledge might be, based on various types of interests and skills.

EXAMPLES OF WHAT YOUR SPECIFIC KNOWLEDGE COULD BE:

MUSICAL TALENTS	THE ABILITY TO PICK UP ANY INSTRUMENT
SALES SKILLS	THE ABILITY TO BE PITHY AND PERSUASIVE
OBSESSIVE PERSONALITY	YOU UNDERSTAND GAME THEORY PRETTY WELL
PLAYING A LOT OF GAMES	THE ABILITY TO DIVE DEEP INTO THINGS AND REMEMBER THEM QUICKLY
ANALYTICAL SKILLS	THE ABILITY TO ABSORB DATA, OBSESS ABOUT IT, AND BREAK IT DOWN
LOVE FOR SCIENCE FICTION	YOU ABSORB A LOT OF KNOWLEDGE VERY QUICKLY

It's important to clarify that *specific* knowledge is not necessarily the same as *specialized* knowledge.

Specialized knowledge means going beyond the fundamentals into the technical. Certainly, specific knowledge may include specialized knowledge, but it often involves much more. It's about figuring out what you bring to the world that no one else can offer. As Naval Ravikant says:

Figure out what you were doing as a kid or teenager almost effortlessly. Something you didn't even consider a skill, but people around you noticed. Your mother or your best friend growing up would know.[6]

For example, consider Dr. House from the hit TV series, *House*. Anyone can memorize different diseases and disorders—that's *specialized* knowledge. What's unique about House is:

- His knack for understanding human behavior (experience taught him that everyone lies).
- His compulsion to solve puzzles and explain the world.
- His comfort with taking risks to do so.

Now *that's* specific knowledge.

More often than not, specific knowledge is not about a lot of knowledge of one particular thing. Usually, it's a *knowledge stack*—a deep understanding of how multiple things connect.

For example, someone might develop specific knowledge about posting super engaging videos about philosophy on YouTube. In this case, the specific knowledge isn't simply about videography. It's about combining knowledge of cameras, great ideas from history, and digital marketing to make something great for people to enjoy.

So, how do we help kids find and develop their specific knowledge stack?

Specialized knowledge is about figuring out what you bring to the world that no one else can offer.

Helping Kids Develop Specific Knowledge

First, it's important to keep in mind that specific knowledge is not about creating child prodigies. It's about helping kids discover their curiosities, gifts, and skills, and creating opportunities for them to have fun stretching their many muscles.

Many people who master specific knowledge are late bloomers, but they spent their "wasted time" figuring out something infinitely important: They know what they can offer the world that no one else can.

Second, we can't force kids to develop specific knowledge.

Kids need a general knowledge about how to learn, how the world works, and how to solve problems.

This is true by definition. In Naval's words, specific knowledge is "what feels like play to you but work to everybody else." Once it starts feeling like work, it's no longer specific knowledge.

That means we must resist the urge to take charge and create a strict process for kids. We can encourage and guide children, but we cannot try to control them. This is a journey they must walk for themselves.

However, they don't have to walk it alone. We can partner with them by:

- Giving them space to dive into what interests them.
- Helping them understand how their unique skills, traits, and interests can help others.
- Talking about how they can apply their specific knowledge to real, complex problems.

Lastly, kids need a strong foundation. They need range, or a general knowledge about how to learn, how the world works, and how to solve problems. They also need exposure to many different subjects, types of work, and life experiences. This will help them discover the things they like best and figure out which ones they have a knack for.

Put another way, kids can't zero in on their specific knowledge unless they've seen the broad swath of opportunities available to them.

But in order to experience these opportunities, they need to embrace...

17

The Art
of Failing
& Quitting

W E'RE TAUGHT IN school that *quitters never win*. While it's true that the ability to persevere when something is difficult can be a competitive advantage, so can knowing when to quit.

We're also taught to fear getting things wrong. Red ink, capital Fs, stern talks after class, and bad report cards. As educator John Holt explains in his book *How Children Fail*, the whole school system was designed to make kids scared of failing.[1]

We have it all backward.

In this chapter, we'll talk about the power of failing and quitting. In sum, we should encourage kids to take risks, get things wrong, try again, and move on when their talents are better used somewhere else. In the right context, allowing kids to fail and quit gives them room to experiment, unlock insights, and dive into new subjects without fear.

Let's begin by looking at the art of failure.

The Art of Failure

Failure should be something we encourage, not punish. Our society needs failure to fuel discovery and progress. We have to try many different things that don't work before we can find the things that do.

Consider the history of science. At first glance, it looks like an unbroken string of success after success, but that's not the case. It's actually about people embracing failure and learning from mistakes.[2]

One good example is the theory of gravity. For around two thousand years, the common belief was that Aristotle was right: things fall at speeds proportional to their weight. Then, Galileo ran experiments and realized that objects move toward the ground at the same acceleration. Newton thought this was because large objects (like the earth) attract smaller objects (like rocks). But Einstein realized that Newton wasn't exactly right. Large objects don't attract smaller objects. Instead, they bend the fabric of space-time. To this day, we're not sure how gravity works at the quantum level, and it will take many more failures before we finally figure out the precise answer.

> The best way to avoid catastrophic failure as an adult is to make lots of small failures as a kid.

If failure feels frightening or foreign, then kids will not venture out. But if failure feels like an old friend, they'll be comfortable trying crazy new ideas. As Naval Ravikant has said:

> No progress is possible without trial and error. Not in business, not in science, not in nature. Without failure, there is no learning, no progress, and no success.[3]

Of course, not all failure helps kids. We don't want our kids to fail to find work, meaning, or happiness, for example. That's catastrophic failure—the type of failure we should help them avoid at all costs.

And the best way to avoid catastrophic failure as an adult is to make lots of small failures as a kid. As Stuart Firestein, professor of biology at Columbia University, says, "We must make and defend a space for non catastrophic failure."[4] It's from small failures that we learn to avoid mistakes with life-altering consequences.

SCALE OF FAILURE

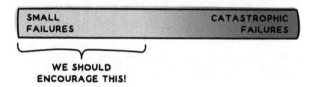

So, how can we help kids fail in ways that are helpful, not hurtful?

Five Ways to Help Kids Fail Constructively

First, give kids lots of opportunities for small failures. Video games are fantastic for giving kids lots of opportunities for small failures because they reframe the learning process. When kids don't get penalized for small mistakes, they feel motivated to pick themselves up, stick with a task, and keep learning. For more on the productive use of video games, see chapter 12: The Psychology of Healthy Gaming.

Second, celebrate failures as opportunities to start again. Frame failure as an exciting quest for feedback. You could ask questions like:

- "What did you learn?"
- "What are you going to try differently next time?"
- "Are you ready to try again, this time with more information?"

"We should encourage kids to take risks, get things wrong, try again, and move on when their talents are better used somewhere else."

Third, encourage the right kind of self-talk. When things go wrong, how do they describe the situation? Watch out for statements like: "This is all my fault. It's going to last forever and ruin everything. There's nothing I can do about it." This pattern can lead to learned helplessness, a psychological state where people feel powerless and trapped.[5]

Try reframing the situation: "This won't last for long. Besides, some parts did work! Don't be so hard on yourself. What do you think you could do to help things go better in the future?"

Fourth, share your own failures with them. Set a positive example by opening up about your own failures and how you handle them. Talk about how you picked yourself up, persevered through difficulty, and learned from your mistakes. Kids learn a lot about how to handle failure by watching adults.[6]

Fifth, talk about heroes who used failure to succeed. Think about the heroes or role models your kids look up to. Make sure they acknowledge the struggles as much as the successes. Pay special attention to the books your kids are reading. Do the main characters always easily win the day? Find stories where the heroes face extreme adversity, stumble, pick themselves up, and achieve success with what they learned from failure.

We've seen that failure should be something we embrace, not penalize.

But what about quitting?

The Art of Quitting

Sometimes, it's okay to give up.

I first saw quitting in this new light when I heard Professor Deepak Malhotra's speech to the 2012 class of Harvard Business

School. His advice was: "Quit early, quit often—not because it's hard, but because it sucks."[7]

Malhotra made a great point: quitting allows you to "say no to a lot of things and yes to the few things that maybe you didn't even know were perfect for you."[8]

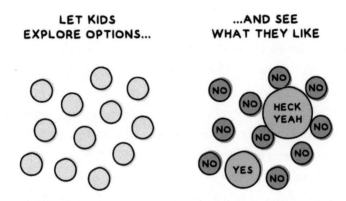

LET KIDS EXPLORE OPTIONS...

...AND SEE WHAT THEY LIKE

We should not quit just because something is difficult, but we should quit when we're going in the wrong direction.

So, how do we help kids learn when to have grit and when to quit?

We've talked about why kids should learn to pursue specific knowledge: those skills they're naturally good at and love to do. We also talked about range: the importance of kids trying many different things to build a foundation and explore their interests.

Quitting is the linchpin between range and specific knowledge.

It's the art of trying new things, realizing what you hate or have no talent for, and moving closer to your specific knowledge. As child psychiatrist and mother-of-three Kristin Levitan puts it:

Giving our kids the option to quit celebrates the idea that they should have the chance to try out new things without the expectation that every new thing will fit.[9]

In addition to encouraging kids to try a variety of things, we also need to teach them *how* and *when* to quit unfulfilling activities.

One tactic is to make principles to help them distinguish between good and bad reasons to stop something.

For example, as a teacher, I made a list of reasons why students might choose to abandon a book:

WHEN IS IT OK TO ABANDON A BOOK?

DISAPPOINTING SEQUEL — NOT APPROPRIATE — TOO CHALLENGING — YOU'RE NOT LEARNING ANYTHING NEW — YOU WEREN'T HOOKED — TOO SCARY — YOU DON'T LIKE THE STYLE — YOU NEED A BREAK — YOU WOULD RATHER LEARN SOMETHING ELSE — TOO CONFUSING — IT'S BORING — YOU WANT TO TRY IT AGAIN IN THE FUTURE — IT'S NOT EXCITING — TOO EASY — IT'S MOVING TOO SLOW — YOU DON'T CONNECT WITH IT

The result? My students stuck to books more often! They abandoned a few along the way, but once they found ones they liked, they couldn't put them down. I started to hear them talk about the rewards of reading and how much more they enjoyed books when they had freedom to find what excites them.

At the start of a new activity (a sport, an after-school program, a book), have kids make a similar list of the conditions under which to quit. Make it clear why they shouldn't quit ("I'm not good enough") and why they should ("I'd rather learn something else").

This method places them in the driver's seat, encouraging them to take ownership over their choices and develop a sense of self-efficacy, but it also provides guidance so they learn how to make thoughtful decisions.

At the end of the day, perseverance and quitting are equally important. As parents and teachers, we shouldn't teach kids to always do one or the other. Instead, we should aim to help kids develop the serenity to stay with the things they're stuck with, the courage to quit the things they aren't stuck with, and the wisdom to know the difference.

Failing and quitting are important parts of genuine learning. In the right context, we should encourage both experiences, not punish them.

The One Question to Avoid

"What do you want to be when you grow up?" is one of the most useless questions an adult can ask a child.

We should not quit just because something is difficult, but we should quit when we're going in the wrong direction.

First, it fosters the wrong kind of mindset by encouraging kids to define themselves in terms of a career and a single identity. As former First Lady Michelle Obama says, we're acting "as if growing up is finite. As if at some point you become something and that's the end."[10] The question suggests that they should have everything already figured out and discourages experimentation, trial and error, and failing and quitting.

Second, what if their ideal job hasn't been invented yet? Old industries are changing. Roughly two-thirds of today's grade-school students will end up doing work that hasn't been invented yet.[11] On the other hand, new industries are emerging faster than ever. Who would have thought it would be possible to make a living out of making YouTube videos? Help kids see that their future self doesn't exist right now and that their interests may change over time.

> Roughly two-thirds of today's grade-school students will end up doing work that hasn't been invented yet.

Third, what if they want to do more than one thing? According to the Bureau of Labor Statistics, the average person ends up holding a dozen different jobs in their lifetime.[12] Teach kids that they don't have to do or be one thing. They can do many things. Teach them to explore a lot of different activities to find out what they are best at and what they enjoy most. Teach them that it's ok to rethink their chosen line of work and switch gears when necessary.

Professor Adam Grant suggests that kids might be better off learning about careers as actions to take rather than identities to claim. When kids see work as what they do rather than who they are, they're more willing to explore different possibilities. For example, in the book *Think Again*, a study showed that when second- and third-graders learned about "doing science" instead of "being a scientist" they were more excited about pursuing a career in science.[13] In Grant's words, "Becoming a scientist might seem out of reach, but the act of experimenting is something we can all try out."[14]

Instead of asking kids what they want to be when they grow up, have them brainstorm about all the things they love to do. Talk to them about careers and professions as something we do rather than someone we are. And make sure they understand that, sometimes, quitting is okay, instead of persevering in the wrong direction.

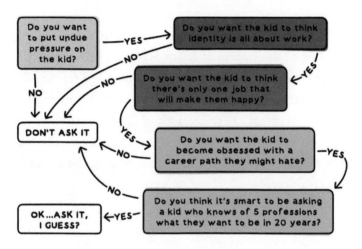

FROM THINK AGAIN BY ADAM GRANT

We shouldn't look down on kids for failing and quitting, as they're both necessary for growth. But that doesn't mean we shouldn't try to help kids improve when we see them struggling.

Perhaps the hardest part of parenting is striking the right balance. As we've seen over the last few chapters, raising successful kids is all about exposing them to difficulties and risks, but not overwhelming them too much. It's about helping them build a general range of skills, but also helping them find their specific knowledge. It's about allowing kids to try new things, fail, and quit, but persevere once they've discovered unique opportunities for them.

How can parents balance all of these together? We need some organizing principles that help us weigh opportunities, keep things in perspective, and prepare our kids for long-term success.

Put another way, we need to learn what it means to become…

Teach kids that they don't have to do or be one thing. Teach them that it's ok to rethink their chosen line of work and switch gears when necessary.

The
Model
Parent

———————

18

Mental Models for Parents

ARLENE WAS AN experienced registered nurse with many years under her belt working in her hospital's Newborn Intensive Care Unit.[1] One day, she walked past an incubator and noticed the baby inside. The baby's designated nurse watched the child routinely without any concern. All of the monitors showed normal vital signs for the newborn. But Darlene felt like something was wrong.

The baby's skin wasn't quite the right color of pink. Its stomach was slightly distended. On its foot, there was a large splotch of red where the child had been pricked to draw blood, showing it hadn't clotted as normal.

Darlene immediately went to the attending physician and requested antibiotics. The doctor wasn't too worried. Each of these pieces of data on its own didn't necessarily mean anything was wrong. But the physician trusted Darlene's instincts, ordered the medicine, and ran tests.

As it turns out, the baby was in the early stages of sepsis, a case of whole-body inflammation from an infection. If Darlene hadn't caught the sickness early, the baby could have died.

The baby's designated nurse had been looking at each piece of information in isolation. Heart rate. Blood pressure. Oxygen levels. Temperature. None of these allowed her to identify the worrying pattern. But Darlene used a mental model. She had a picture in her head of what a healthy baby looks like, and compared this individual newborn to that general model.

As researcher Beth Crandall put it:

> To the other nurse, the mottled skin and the bloody Band-Aid were data points, nothing big enough to trigger an alarm. But Darlene put everything together. She saw a whole picture.[2]

In this chapter, we'll discuss the nature of mental models. We'll look at specific examples that are relevant to parents, and unpack how parents can integrate these into their daily lives. By the end, I hope that you will recognize the power of mental models for parenting, feel comfortable using them yourself, and get excited about diving deeper and finding new models on your own.

But first, let's clarify exactly what mental models are.

What Are Mental Models?

Put simply, mental models are general rules of thumb about how the world works. They empower us to organize our experiences into something that makes sense.

Think about it this way. When you visit a new town, you might see a McDonald's on your left, a bank on your right, and a Walmart straight ahead. On their own, these bits of information don't mean very much, but if you have a map that charts these landmarks, you can figure out where you are and make a plan to move forward.

Mental models work like maps for life. They help us make

connections, recognize patterns, and gain a higher-level perspective so we can make good decisions.

As author James Clear says, "The phrase 'mental model' is an overarching term for any sort of concept, framework, or worldview that you carry around in your mind."[3] Moreover, mental models aren't optional. Instead, they're "critical for anyone interested in thinking clearly, rationally, and effectively."[4]

Every discipline has mental models. Biology. Physics. Economics. Psychology. Each field uses general principles that apply in many different situations. But unlike the details of scientific research, mental models are not hard to master. They're the most basic ideas from each discipline that we can learn to help us understand the fundamentals of life.

Consider the idea of critical mass. In nuclear engineering, it means the smallest amount of uranium or plutonium needed to create a nuclear chain reaction. But this idea applies to many other things besides nuclear engineering. You could also use the mental model of critical mass for thousands of other things: the smallest number of customers necessary to support a business, and the smallest number of books you need to read to understand World War II. Ideas can attain critical mass, and so can a party.

Mental models work like maps for life.

Or think about Newton's first law of physics: objects in motion will stay in motion unless acted upon by another force. Obviously, this applies to physical things, like rockets in space, which will continue on their trajectory once you launch them beyond earth's gravity. But it also applies to people more generally. If I watch four hours of Netflix every day, I will probably continue to watch four hours of Netflix a day, unless I find a reason to do something more productive.

To understand the world, we need many different mental models. Investor Charlie Munger puts it this way: "The models have to come from multiple disciplines—because all the wisdom of the world is not to be found in one little academic department… You've got to have models across a fair array of disciplines."[5]

We need these mental models because "if the facts don't hang together on a latticework of theory, you don't have them in usable form."[6] Only with mental models can we put information and our experiences together in a way that we can use them to make good decisions.

Mental models are especially helpful when we face complex situations. When new information hits us left and right, we need to know how to interpret it. We need a guiding light to lead us in the right direction when things get chaotic.

This is particularly true with parenting.

Our kids change every day. They're leaping from one stage of development to another. And we're overloaded with all sorts of data, from the opinion of your mother-in-law and the newest hot tip on your favorite mommy blog, to the latest findings of childhood psychology.

What should we do with it all?

Without mental models, it's easy to get overwhelmed and paralyzed, but with mental models, you can sort the good ideas from the bad, orient yourself to what's most important, and take decisive action.

Let's look at five mental models that could be helpful for parents.

"

We need a variety of tools at our disposal to meet kids where they are and help them adapt to their latest challenges.

"

Mental Models for Parents

Maslow's Hammer

The psychologist Abraham Maslow once said, "If the only tool you have is a hammer, it is tempting to treat everything as if it were a nail."[7] It's very easy for parents to fall into this trap. We learn one tactic and start to see every problem in that light. When our kids misbehave, maybe we think they haven't had enough punishments, need more rewards, more well-behaved friends, or some other pat solution.

The truth is that when kids start acting out of character, they probably need something new, not more of the same. Each stage of their young life is unique. They're growing, developing, changing, and facing new situations. We need a variety of tools at our disposal to meet kids where they are and help them adapt to their latest challenges.

Reactance

The more we're pressured to do something, the less we want to do it. We might enjoy running, but as soon as our PE teacher makes us run, it feels miserable. Psychologists call this *reactance*.[8]

Humans naturally want choice and autonomy—and that goes for kids too. If you really want your child to do something, but they continue to fight against you, ask yourself whether you've given them a choice.

It's counterintuitive, but giving kids autonomy to participate is often the fastest way to a positive solution for both of you.

Nudges

When we want our kids to change their behavior, we feel like the first step is to convince them of something. Maybe we want them to eat healthy food, so we talk about the importance of fruits. But talking about a healthy diet isn't enough. We also need to partner with them to design an environment where it's easier for them to make the best choice. Social scientists call this a *nudge*: a simple change in the context that makes good choices easier than bad choices.[9]

For example, you might ask yourself, "How can I make it easier for them to reach fruit instead of candy?" By making apples and bananas more accessible, you can help them choose natural sugars over processed sugars.

Now, the topic of your conversations with them is different. You're not simply saying that fruit is better than candy. You're also talking about how they can help themselves develop better lifelong habits. You can discuss with them the benefits of making fruit easier to reach than candy so that when they grow up, they have the skills to set themselves up for a healthy life.

Reframing

When kids face a crisis, it's often an issue of *framing*. They've framed the problem in a negative way, but with a new perspective, they can see the positives.

Maybe they're sad because they can't spend the night at their grandparents' house, but we can help them look at the situation from a different angle. We can encourage them to use that evening time to write a letter to their grandparents, or make a craft and surprise them the next day. With the extra time, they have the chance for a new creative project.

Author Thomas Wedell-Wedellsborg calls this *reframing*.[10]

Reframing gives us a way to help kids realize that they often can't control life—but they can control how they respond to it. Kids can choose to be sad, or seize the day and turn the bad situation into something good.

Inversion

When faced with a tough problem, it often helps to look at it from the opposite perspective. Investor Charlie Munger calls this mental model *inversion*. Here's how he describes it:

> Problems frequently get easier if you turn them around in reverse. In other words, if you want to help India, the question you should ask is not 'how can I help India,' it's 'what is doing the worst damage in India and how do I avoid it?'

Entrepreneur and investor Andrew Wilkinson used inversion to come up with *anti-goals:* a strategy to help you focus on what you don't want so you can work out what you do want.[11] For example, he realized that he didn't want days filled with long meetings, so he set the goal, "Never schedule an in-person meeting when it can otherwise be accomplished via email or phone (or not at all)." He also realized that he didn't want to work with people who he did not trust, so he set the goal, "No business or obligations with people we don't like—even just a slight bad vibe and it's a hard no." Instead of focusing on what he wanted, he started with what he didn't want, and then he worked backward.

I've found this is an especially helpful exercise to do with my students. Most kids have no idea what they want. If you ask them, "What do you want to accomplish this year?", they have no clue how to respond. However, if you ask them what they don't want to do, they'll easily give you a long list!

You can use this list to clarify the things that make them unhappy and plan specific steps they can implement to ensure they won't happen. So have them list the things they don't enjoy doing or what makes them unhappy, and then list the specific steps they will implement to ensure these won't happen (anti-goals). By keeping in mind what to avoid, it's easier to know what to do.

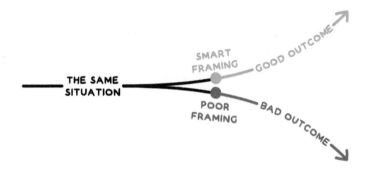

Building Your Own Mental Models

Together, these five mental models can help parents make sense of complex scenarios. When things get chaotic with kids, we can ask:

- Am I trying to use the wrong tool here (Maslow's hammer)?
- Am I trying to force something onto my kids without giving them a voice (reactance)?
- How can I encourage them in the right direction (nudges)?

• Or maybe they need me to help them see the situation from a different perspective (reframing and inversion)?

These models are only five of hundreds of other tools parents can use to help them raise their kids. Let's look at some other tactics and resources to help build out your own mental models.

First, check out Farnam Street. This is an organization run by Shane Parrish, focused on helping people learn and use the best of mental-model thinking. They provide helpful resources on their blog and in their books, and even offer a course on mental models for parenting.[12]

Second, read *Super Thinking*. This is a book written by Gabriel Weinberg, the founder and CEO of DuckDuckGo, and his wife Lauren McCann.[13] Together, they walk through well over 100 mental models and how they apply to real life.

Third, start practicing. Using mental models effectively is all about practice. When you see your child act a certain way, ask whether you've seen the pattern before. Try to connect the dots, make generalizations with other things you've experienced, and see if any commonalities exist.

It often helps to look at a problem from the opposite perspective.

Fourth, keep notes on your child's behavior. It's helpful to have some documentation to reference with your child. Take a few minutes to note the things you realized, and what happened as a result. This will give you a resource to refer back to and allow you to find some of the longer-term patterns with your kids. Over time, this will also help you develop some mental models specific to your children.

Fifth, use checklists. Even when we recognize common patterns, it's hard to remember the right actions to take. Try testing out some checklists.[14] For example, when your child refuses to go to bed on time, you might create a list of things to try. With enough experimentation, you can find the tactics that work, keep using them while they're effective, and update them as your child grows and develops new patterns.

With mental models, we can reduce the complexity of parenting. We can use a few rules of thumb to organize our experience, give us insight, and map the right way forward.

But mental models aren't the only tools available for us to think well about the things we face in life. In the next chapter, we'll cover a few more, as we unpack...

19

The Thinking Toolkit

NTELLIGENCE MEANS POTENTIAL for good thinking—but many intelligent people never seize upon their potential. They never learn *how to think*.

By contrast, many people are excellent thinkers, even without much natural talent. They had good teachers and practiced a lot. As psychologist Edward de Bono wrote, intelligence is like a car:

A powerful car may be driven badly. A less powerful car may be driven well. The skill of the car driver determines how the power of the car is used.

In other words, good thinking isn't exactly an innate trait. Instead, it's better to view it as a set of learned skills that nearly anyone can develop with deliberate practice.

In this chapter, we will consider three different kinds of thinking tools: thinking hats, thinking in bets, and elastic thinking. Primarily, we'll talk about these tactics as skills that we can teach to our children, but they're much broader than that. They're techniques that everyone can use to improve their thinking processes and decision-making abilities.

Let's begin by discussing six different *thinking hats*.

The Thinking Hats

Good thinking is the skill of putting all the available information to the best use possible. It's about more than critical thinking, logic, and analysis. It includes these tools, but it also includes creativity, exploration, design, and perception. The best thinkers use all sorts of tactics.

So, how do you learn to think? And how do you teach your kids?

Edward de Bono wrote a great book, *Teach Your Child How To Think*, in which he shares how parents can teach their kids to use different "thinking hats."[2] Each hat represents a different perspective that we can take when we're thinking through a problem. Each of them are different and help us to see things from a distinctive point of view.

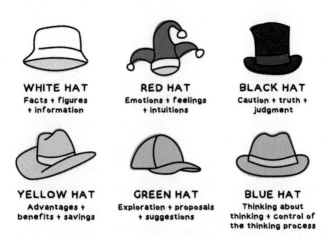

WHITE HAT
Facts + figures + information

RED HAT
Emotions + feelings + intuitions

BLACK HAT
Caution + truth + judgment

YELLOW HAT
Advantages + benefits + savings

GREEN HAT
Exploration + proposals + suggestions

BLUE HAT
Thinking about thinking + control of the thinking process

Let's discuss each of the hats in turn.

First, the white hat represents facts, figures, and information. This hat focuses on the available information and seeks objective facts, not what anyone feels about them. When you are wearing the white hat, you may ask questions like, "What information do I have? What information is missing? How do I get the information I need?"

Second, the red hat represents emotions, feelings, hunches, and intuitions. It's the opposite of the white hat. The red hat is not interested in facts, but rather in people's feelings. When you are wearing the red hat you may ask yourself, "What do I feel about this situation right now? How might this situation make others feel?"

Third, the black hat represents caution, truth, and judgment. It's the hat of critical thinking. De Bono says you can think of a stern judge or a teacher who gives you a red mark if you get something wrong. When you are wearing the black hat, you may ask questions like, "Is it true? Does it fit the facts? Will it work? Is it safe? Can it be done?"

The black hat is often overused in traditional school and work settings. But when used in combination with other hats, it prevents us from making silly mistakes and can lead to the improvement of ideas.

Fourth, the yellow hat represents advantages, benefits, and savings. Think of sunshine and optimism. This hat is full of hope, but it's also a logical hat, so the reasons behind the hope must be provided. When you are wearing the yellow hat you may say things like, "This is why it can be done, why there are benefits, and why it is a good thing to do."

Fifth, the green hat represents exploration, proposals, suggestions, and new ideas. Think of the energy of growth, fertility, and vegetation. This is the hat for creativity, thinking outside of the box, and putting new ideas on the table. When you put on the green hat, you may make suggestions like, "Ok, this might sound crazy, but what if we try this instead."

Sixth, the blue hat represents thinking about thinking. Think of the blue sky above everything. With the blue thinking hat, you are looking *over* the thinking process from a high-level perspective. De Bono says it's like the conductor of the orchestra. With all the other hats, we think about the subject matter itself, but with the blue hat, we think about how we're using the other thinking hats. For example, we're using the blue hat in this chapter!

When you wear the blue hat, you might ask questions like, "What assumption are we making? Are we spending enough time using the red hat? Should we be more creative? What's the next step?"

Too often, we act like the white hat (facts) and black hat (judgment) are the only valuable perspectives. But good thinkers use *all six hats*. They also consider their emotions, evaluate upsides, propose crazy ideas, and monitor their overall thinking process.

The six hats help kids see with a *wide-angle lens*. Kids learn to broaden their perception and use a diverse set of mental skills. In other words, they build wisdom.

The best thinkers use all sorts of tactics.

Wisdom is the ultimate goal of good thinking. It's the habit of observing the breadth of a situation. Unlike intelligence, wisdom is not a natural-born talent. It's also not the natural product of age. We've all met wise kids and foolish adults! Wisdom comes from deliberate practice. It requires mentorship and experience in solving complex problems. With training in how to use these six hats, kids can build more wisdom in a year than many adults learn their entire lives!

After using each of the hats, you might determine that you

can't tell exactly how things will turn out. What do you do in this situation?

In the next section, we'll talk about how to bring probabilities into the equation.

Thinking in Bets

Great thinkers are also great gamblers. They constantly make bets and use probabilities. Let's talk about why this habit makes such a big difference, and how to help kids use good decision-making processes.

Tough choices require *prospective thinking*.[3] They make us consider the future. Marriage, voting, investing, parenting, jobs— all the important decisions in life force us to think about how things will unfold.

The problem? The future isn't certain.

In ten years, the world will look much different than any of us or our kids can imagine. So, how do we make good choices when none of us are sure how things will play out?

First, let's do an exercise created by Annie Duke, former professional poker player and author of one of my favorite books, *Thinking in Bets*.[4]

Think about your best decision last year.

Got it? Good.

How did that decision turn out?

- Good
- Bad
- Average

"

Encourage kids to think in probabilities, not absolutes. The faster they learn that the future may go in many different directions, the better.

"

If you're like most people, then you picked a decision that ended well. Why? Because we tend to judge choices based on outcomes. When I asked you to think about your best decision, you were probably already thinking about a decision that turned out well!

But that's a problem that Annie Duke calls *resulting.*[5]

In *Thinking in Bets,* she uses the example of the Seahawks in the 2015 Super Bowl. Coach Carroll called for a pass at the end of the game. The Patriots intercepted and won. So many people hated Coach Carroll because of the bad ending, but it was actually a good choice. In 15 seasons, only 2% of passes were intercepted in that situation.[6]

We shouldn't use results to judge our decisions. Luck plays too big of a role. Instead, we should focus on what we can control. We should focus on our decision-making process.

So, how can we help our kids use good decision-making processes? Let's discuss four lessons that every kid should learn and every adult should remember.

First, encourage them to think in probabilities, not absolutes. We all naturally think in black and white, but life is much more complicated. Encourage kids to resist saying things like "that's guaranteed." Instead, ask them to use percentages to express the likelihood of different outcomes. The faster they learn that the future may go in many different directions, the better!

Second, help them keep their minds open. As decision scientist Philip Tetlock says, great decision makers are like foxes —they're nimble, flexible, and adaptable.[7] It's easy to always use one big idea to interpret the world, but help kids to practice the opposite. Use the six thinking hats to encourage them to see things from many different perspectives before they settle on an answer.

Third, let kids work together in groups. Even our kids have biases that they can't escape on their own. The solution? Put them into teams with their friends! Spur them to point out mistakes they see in each other. Let them ask hard questions and hold each other accountable.

Fourth, allow them to update their beliefs. Instead of penalizing them when they get things wrong, we should let kids treat each decision as a little test. They should be asking themselves things like, "How did that go? What did I learn? How can I improve next time?" without any concern about whether or not an adult agrees with them.

Of course, some choices are too big for us to let kids experiment with them, but for many daily decisions, it's safe to give kids the chance to try things out, get things wrong, learn, and improve their thinking.

As we've seen, we should think in bets when we're trying to make decisions about the future—but what about when we're trying to *create* the future? How should we think about the world when we're innovating and inventing?

Elastic Thinking

In many ways, humans are not that special. Chimps are stronger than us, pound for pound. And some jellyfish are immortal! But there's a special way we *think* that makes us so unique. It empowers us to build cities, invent new technology, and go to the moon.

You might be wondering: "But don't animals think too? They have brains, after all." But it's the special *way we think* that matters.

Leonard Mlodinow, physicist and colleague of Richard Feynman, distinguishes between three kinds of thinking:

1. **Automatic**: reflexive responses to situations.
2. **Analytical**: careful analytical analysis.
3. **Elastic**: creative, spontaneous connections.[8]

Most animals only use the first kind of thinking: reflexive responses to situations. Think about the herring gull. When a parent taps the ground, it triggers them to barf, and its chicks run over and start pecking. That's automatic thinking! They're following natural reflexes.

We use automatic thinking too. For example, we naturally reciprocate generosity. We give to people who give to us. Salespeople take advantage of this reflex. They might send us a small gift so it's easier to sell us a car.

But we can escape this trap. How? By never accepting gifts from salespeople.[9] If we create this rule and always follow it, we'll never fall for that trick again. This tactic is an example of the second kind of thinking: analytical.

Traditional education focuses mostly on teaching analytical thinking. Kids are taught to use logic to make plans, calculate answers, and change their automatic behaviors. Computers use analytical thinking too. In fact, they're much better at it than any kid—and even the smartest adults! For example, the computer Deep Blue beat reigning chess champion Garry Kasparov in 1996.[10] Now, computers beat chess champions all the time!

Computers perfectly follow logical steps. They do exactly what we tell them to do. However, they break down when they face new situations. They can't use the third kind of thinking: elastic.

Elastic thinking helps people solve problems humanity

has never faced before. It's what we do when we don't have a rulebook to follow. Instead of thinking step by step, we dive into the adventure of exploration and discovery until new solutions click into place.

In Mlodinow's words: automatic thinking helps us drive cars, and analytical thinking helps us build them, but elastic thinking gave Carl Benz the idea of inventing the car in the first place.[11]

ELASTIC THINKING
HELPED INVENT A CAR

ANALYTICAL THINKING
HELPS US BUILD CARS

AUTOMATIC THINKING
HELPS US DRIVE CARS

Elastic thinking is more valuable than ever. In the modern world, things change constantly. New problems arise faster than people can solve the old ones. As a result, we should pivot our approach to education so that it takes a much higher priority than it does in a typical school. Kids need the chance to develop the skill of developing original ideas so that they can create solutions.

So, how do we help kids get better at elastic thinking? The process is straightforward, but it requires us to do the opposite of what traditional schools are doing.

Did you ever hear a teacher say, "Wait until you get into the real world"? That's because school makes life seem too simple. They teach kids that success means:

- Following rules.
- Memorizing pat answers.
- Solving simplified problems.

It's a real tragedy, because this is the opposite of the recipe for success in the real world. Schools suck the novelty out of learning, and kids end up spending their most formative years without practicing elastic thinking.

> Wisdom is the ultimate goal of good thinking and it comes from deliberate practice.

To help kids get better at elastic thinking, we need to flip school on its head.

We need to let kids follow their natural intuition. We must allow them to throw away the instructions, and practice discovery and adventure on their own.

We need to give them opportunities to engage in unstructured play, pursue their own self-directed projects, experiment, and explore possibilities beyond a typical classroom "lesson plan."

You might be surprised at what they'll invent. Kids are capable of much more than we give them credit for, if we let them be.

Design
Your
Learning
Game

———————

O NCE YOU BECOME aware of the game of school, you may feel ready to opt out of it and opt into the game of learning.

Below are a few guidelines to keep in mind as you design a learning game that works for you and your children. I plan to keep these summary takeaways at hand as I build learning experiences with my kids, and I hope they inspire you to do the same.

Stop over-instructing kids so they have space to think creatively and independently. Give kids the chance to figure things out for themselves. Provide the building blocks, then get out of the way and let kids create. As we ask kids to put more of themselves into learning, they'll rise to the challenge and become more engaged and better prepared. Having space to think independently will get them excited about learning.

Reframe the learning process so that kids are not scared of failure. Penalizing failure makes failure frightening. And fear of failure can keep kids from trying. Help kids learn from their mistakes, and encourage them to try again.

Pay attention to the feedback and praise you give. Recognize effort, not ability. Recognize ethics over achievement. Recognize the learning process, not the outcome. Recognize curiosity, perseverance, and a growth mindset over the completion of tasks.

Give kids choices and make them feel accountable. Talk to kids like adults. Involve them when making decisions. Trust them to do things well, even if how they do them isn't exactly what you expect.

Encourage kids to tackle projects of their own. Real learning happens when kids work intensely on things that matter to them. Create the conditions for healthy obsessions to happen.

Broaden the methods by which you measure progress. Give kids multiple ways to show their skills and knowledge. Don't overly focus on tests and grades. What matters is learning how to learn.

Avoid extrinsic motivators. Rewards may help kids reach short-term academic benchmarks or behavior goals, but they distract us from the ultimate goal of raising self-directed, lifelong learners. Unlock intrinsic motivation instead.

Help kids get comfortable with the uncomfortable. If they can embrace difficult feelings, uncertainty, not fitting in, and being unsure, they'll build the internal resources to thrive in the world.

Let kids dwell on their confusion. Resist the urge to jump to the rescue when they get confused. Just the right amount of confusion sparks curiosity and encourages growth. Not enough confusion causes boredom.

Let them question everything. Teach your kids that it's ok to inquire and ask for more evidence before accepting a claim as true. Help kids cultivate an attitude of skepticism. Encourage kids to reject the defaults.

Cherish the "Why?" questions. Kids ask "why" a lot because they're trying to understand how things work. They're trying to deconstruct what's thrown at them to decide if it makes sense. They're trying to think for themselves.

Wrap data, numbers, formulas, and theories around a person with a good story. Kids are more likely to learn and emulate when they emotionally connect to someone.

Help them develop character like the Stoics: courageous, just, temperate, and wise. True education isn't just about learning how to get ahead. It's about how to live a meaningful, moral life. Share stories of true heros, help kids focus on how to respond calmly and respectfully, and encourage them to use a virtue journal that keeps track of how they're living these values.

Don't make kids memorize information they can google. Focus on helping kids understand *why* information is important, *how* we know it's true, and *how* they can apply concepts on their own. When they do need to memorize, ditch flash cards and help them build a memory palace.

Help kids figure out how to play to their strengths. They need to try a range of activities, quit what does not fit, iterate, explore, and find their specific knowledge—their obsessions, talents, and natural skills.

Intelligence is different from skilled thinking. Good thinking is a collection of skills and mindsets that help us see with a wide-angle lens. Help kids learn good thinking perspectives and practice applying them with intention.

Remind kids that they have a big toolbox of ways to learn and that their learning preferences are not fixed. Replace the *one learning style* method with a broad base of mental models kids can use to make sense of the world, make better decisions, and problem-solve.

Video games can be tools for learning. They're interactive, there's not much at stake if you lose, and they allow you to learn from failure and get better.

Kids find online what they miss in school. They get to spend time on what interests them online. If they play games, they decide how to play them and who to play them with. They connect with like-minded people.

However, screen addiction is a real problem. Have real conversations about what they get out of screen time, and find ways to find these rewards in the real world. Manage it together instead of just setting a hard limit.

Gamify learning, but don't turn it into point-gathering games. Create goals kids are already invested in, challenge them just enough to keep things interesting, give them clear and applicable feedback, and let them try again. Unlike stickers and recess time, games built with this thinking create a flow state.

Help kids increase the stakes of learning. Tie concepts to high-stakes scenarios that mirror reality without the possibility of life-changing failure.

Deeply engage in your child's learning. Don't just drop them off at school and hope for the best. Getting involved will give them a sense of stability and give you a role filling in any gaps in their learning. You'll come to understand how to best partner with them to encourage their learning. Enjoy this time learning and growing together.

Use mental models to understand your child's behavior so you can react to it in a healthy way. Mental models are maps we can use to make sense of the complexity of raising kids. They help us diagnose problems and take action that's likely to create positive outcomes. It's important to recognize the specific patterns in your child's life and create your own model for healthy ways to respond.

The line is thin between well-meaning actions and *overprotection*. Your child can handle more than you think. They can grow stronger when they're challenged.

Find balance. Challenging children is helpful until it isn't. It's important to have stakes, but not life-altering ones. Let them get comfortable with failure, but learn when they need support. Help them persevere when it matters and quit when it doesn't.

These guiding principles boil down to a key idea: kids are capable of way more than you think. You just need to create room for them to show you and the world.

As an adult, you still have a role. You need to help create a framework that makes sense for your child. It isn't easy, but it's worth it.

No one can get it completely right all the time. But just by being interested and engaged in your child's education, you've taken the first step towards helping them play a different game. One that invests in them, encourages their own investment, teaches them how to think, and prepares them for the real world.

Just trying a few of these guidelines will help you pivot from traditional education to a place of exploration, critical thinking, independence, creativity, nimbleness, and skin in the game.

That's what I call *real learning.*

Resources

How to Exit the System (Without Leaving School)

OFTEN TALK with parents who feel trapped. They see the major problems with the traditional system, but they aren't in a place where they can take their kids out of school. They want something better for their kids, but homeschooling takes lots of time.

The good news is that there are other options that can give kids an off-ramp out of the system.

In this section, we will walk through eight different ways kids can exit the traditional system without leaving school. Each of the options shares common traits. Although they are unique, they all take *Lindy ideas* from the past and apply them to today in various ways.

First, what's a Lindy idea?

The Lindy Effect

In his book *Antifragile*, Nassim Taleb describes the Lindy Effect. In essence, it says that ideas age differently than people. The longer ideas have been around, the longer they're likely to last.

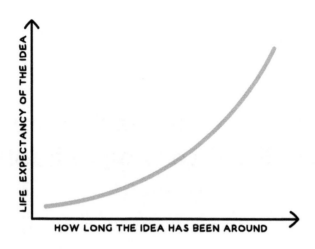

Lindy ideas stick around for a reason: they often work quite well. We may not always know why they work, but that shouldn't discourage us from taking them seriously. We should leverage wisdom from the past and adapt those lessons for today.

Let's look at five examples in education.

First, play is Lindy. Free play is our natural method of learning about the world. Since ancient times, we've used it to explore, experiment, and build new knowledge by venturing into the unknown.

Forcing kids to sit at desks for six hours a day is not Lindy.

Second, learning by doing is Lindy. Hunter-gatherers let kids learn survival skills through practice. They played with bows, spears, and cooking tools, and participated in the work of the tribe.

Waiting to contribute to the world until college graduation is not Lindy.

Third, the teacher as facilitator is Lindy. Throughout history, the best educators acted as wise guides. Rather than conveying knowledge, they facilitated questions and dialogue until students arrived at their own understanding. It was a collaborative model of truth seeking.

Teaching like an authoritarian who has all the answers is not Lindy.

Fourth, the Socratic method is Lindy. For hundreds of years, teachers used the method of the Greek philosopher Socrates. Instead of lecturing, he asked penetrating questions to help students develop their own beliefs, using their own reasoning.

But aren't lectures also Lindy?

Yes, lectures are Lindy, but for a particular reason. Way before the internet, books and lectures were how we transferred information. They accomplished this goal well for the time, but if you want to engage kids and help them learn, Socratic questions work much better.

Fifth, one-room schoolhouses are Lindy. Historically, kids attended one-room schoolhouses (or "microschools" today) where they learned in small, mixed aged groups. Older kids taught younger kids, and younger kids learned from older ones.

Segregating kids into grades, by age, is not Lindy.

Most schools today do not follow these five Lindy ideas. They separate older and younger kids, limit play and practice, and force kids to listen to teachers who lecture for hours on what they should believe. In short, *schools have fallen into the trap of trying to outsmart Lindy*.

Thankfully, parents have an increasing number of alternative schools and educational programs that they can use to do things differently. They can replace or supplement their kids' traditional education with learning experiences that are grounded in Lindy ideas and updated for today.

Let's look at eight of them.

First, parents can use self-directed learning communities. Programs like Galileo[2] help kids make friends with peers who share their interests and design their own curriculums together. They can learn coding, game design, art, writing, and entrepreneurship in over 100 classes.

Second, parents can use Forest School. Forest School[3] programs put kids at the center, connect them with each other and nature, and challenge them to take responsibility and make meaning for themselves. You can lead Forest School sessions yourself, or sign kids up for a program.

Third, parents can use team problem-solving. Synthesis School[4] empowers kids to solve the world's hardest problems. They compete in teams to win simulations by debating ideas, testing tactics, communicating decisions, taking ownership, and drawing out the best in each other.

Fourth, parents can use project-based learning. Programs like Arduino[5] challenge kids with projects that teach them chemistry, physics, electronics, coding, and more. They ship all the components to your door, provide online training and support, and let kids learn by doing.

Fifth, parents can use online STEAM classes. Many schools struggle to give kids the opportunity to explore their interests in science, tech, engineering, art, and math (STEAM subjects). Thankfully, platforms like Brilliant.org, Skillshare, and Khan Academy offer a plethora of amazing courses on all of these subjects.[6]

Sixth, parents can foster a love for reading. Let kids read freely and widely. Let them try books and abandon them. Let them skim through books, and dive deep into what interests them: poems, comic books, nonfiction, magazines, cookbooks— or even the same book over and over. Choice is the secret recipe to foster a love of reading. And once they develop a love for reading, they'll be able to teach themselves anything.

Seventh, parents can use alternative schools. If you can move your kids into a better school, consider exploring alternative programs based on these methods: Montessori, Waldorf, and Reggio Emilia.[7] For specific alternative schools, you might want to explore Sora Schools, Higher Ground, and Acton Academy.[8]

Eighth, parents can use microschools. Microschools are also wonderful options, like those available through Prenda[9] and other networks. To find a good one, look for these features:

- Mixed age groups.
- Child-centered curriculum.
- Project-based learning.

Look for programs focused on free play, where kids explore and create on their own. Avoid ones that talk about "play," but really mean adult-led activities.

With these eight options, you can create opportunities for your kids to avoid some of the dangerous side effects of modern education, without having to take them out of school. Or you can replace traditional school with an alternative school, or pair traditional school with other educational programs. You'll give kids the freedom to create, play, explore ideas, dive into projects of their own, and make friends with like-minded peers.

Ms. Fab Book Recommendations

N THIS SECTION, I'd like to walk through some of my favorite book recommendations and offer a few thoughts on why these books are so valuable. All three books share a common theme. They're all about how to interact with kids in a way that supports their agency and respects their development stages.

First, we'll explore *How to Raise Successful People* by Esther Wojcicki, then *The Whole-Brain Child* by Drs. Daniel J. Siegel and Tina Payne Bryson, and finally *Never Split the Difference* by Christopher Voss.

Let's dig in.

How to Raise Successful People

Esther Wojcicki is a teacher with 40 years of experience, a Silicon Valley legend, and the mother of three successful daughters: Susan, CEO of YouTube; Anne, CEO of 23andMe; and Janet, a professor at UCSF.

How did Esther raise so many successful kids?

In her best-selling book, *How To Raise Successful People*, Esther says the key is a philosophy called TRICK:

- Trust
- Respect
- Independence
- Collaboration
- Kindness

What parent wouldn't agree with these five values? They seem obvious—and maybe even a little trivial. But what makes Esther's philosophy special is how she applies them in real-life situations. Let's look at some examples.

Trust

Trust means believing kids can figure things out for themselves. For example, one Saturday Esther's grandson (12 years old) needed a haircut and her two granddaughters (eight years old) needed school supplies. But she didn't have time for both trips. So, she dropped her grandson off at the barbershop and let him pick his haircut. And dropped off her granddaughters at Target and let them buy their supplies.

Both are relatively safe places, but to many parents, this still might sound crazy. How will they know what to do?

Esther uses this story to make a powerful point: if we don't trust kids to do things, they won't learn to take care of themselves. They'll turn into adults who aren't confident enough to solve their own problems. But if we give them trust, they learn to trust themselves.

Respect

Respect means supporting kids as they identify and pursue their own goals. Esther's grandson, Jacob, was slow to start walking. At 18 months, he was still scooting around the floor on his bottom. The doctor said his legs worked fine, but his parents still worried.

Jacob loved basketball, so Esther took him to Gymboree. Immediately, he was glued to the other kids dribbling. One kid took a shot, the ball bounced away, and Jacob ran to go take his turn.

Jacob knew how to walk. He just needed a good enough reason to show everyone else. In Esther's words:

> Parents need to calm down. Your kids will walk. They will talk... Kids need to be allowed to take the lead. That means you follow them. Children know who they are. Your job is to honor and respect that.[2]

You can show respect by nurturing your kids' autonomy and individuality.

Independence

Independence means not doing anything for your kids that they can do for themselves. In other words, it means giving kids age-appropriate levels of freedom. That way, they start learning to take care of themselves from their earliest years.

Esther, for example, used the "pause principle" with her newborns. When her babies cried in the night, she would wait a moment before comforting them. This short break gives infants a chance to practice self-soothing and take their first steps toward independence. As Esther says:

> I know this will sound crazy to some people, but here's my ultimate goal as a teacher and parent: to make myself obsolete. That's right. I want kids to be so independent that they no longer need me.[3]

Collaboration

Collaboration means working with kids like partners in crime.

That's how Esther ran her classrooms. Instead of lecturing at students, she let them contribute to discussions, decisions, and even discipline. But the school admin didn't like this model. She shares:

> The rebel in me came up with an unusual idea. I told my students what was happening to me, and that the next time the principal came to evaluate me, they needed to be totally quiet or I was going to be fired. I actually told them that. I trusted them... and I had nothing to lose.[4]

Her idea worked! Ordinarily, the classroom buzzed with collaboration, but when the principal entered, the kids stopped talking, sat still, and Esther gave a lecture. The class got high behavior marks, Esther kept her job, and the students kept their teacher.

Kindness

Kindness means living a life filled with care, warmth, empathy, and concern for others. According to Esther, it's the most important parenting principle. Trust, respect, independence, and collaboration must lead to kids who add more kindness to the world.

Kindness needs two things to grow: examples and practice. Esther taught her daughters with her actions, the books she read, and the shows she recommended. She challenged them to always lend a hand, make eye contact, smile, and offer greetings... small things with huge impact.

Ironically, Esther notes, helicopter parenting tends to sacrifice kindness in favor of personal success. But kindness is key to personal success. Whether you're trying to get into Stanford or Google, recruiters look for candidates who will treat others well.

Esther raised three talented daughters, but their real success isn't their prestigious jobs. What matters most is that they're independent thinkers who can take care of themselves and show kindness to others.

And with TRICK, any parent can raise their kids the same way.

The Whole-Brain Child

All parents have moments of difficulty with their kids. Maybe they're refusing to put on their shoes or get ready for bed. But with the right tactics, you can turn these challenges into opportunities for growth and connection.

In their book, *The Whole-Brain Child*, Drs. Siegel and Bryson share the story of Katie.[5] She used to love school, but after getting sick in class one day, she started to fight her dad tooth and nail every morning. One morning as he dropped her off at school, she yelled at him, "I'll die if you leave me!"

All kids, including Katie, are still learning to coordinate thoughts and feelings. Their behavior might look like defiance, but it's actually them struggling to process situations. And with a little brain science, we can better empathize and guide kids to handle hard things well.

The human brain has four sections:

1. Left brain = **logic**.
2. Right brain = **emotion**.
3. Upstairs brain = **thoughtful**.
4. Downstairs brain = **reactive**.

THE HUMAN BRAIN HAS FOUR SECTIONS:

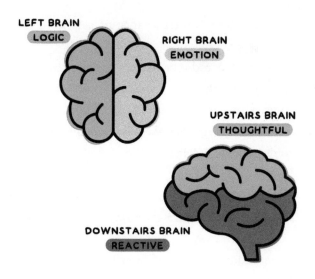

In children, these four sections haven't learned to work together. And when kids' logic, emotions, thoughtfulness, and instincts aren't integrated, it makes it very hard for them to handle difficulties well.

It's like watching a teenage boy play soccer after a big growth spurt. His left leg doesn't know what his right leg is doing—which inevitably leads to a few awkward tumbles.

Katie, for example, struggled to balance her right-brain emotions with her left-brain logic. Or consider Grant, a four-year-old who tried to hit his sister for losing his favorite rock. He struggled to balance his downstairs reaction with his upstairs thoughtfulness. Thankfully, parents have opportunities to help kids grow.

Our brains are incredibly plastic. They rewire themselves as we go through experiences and reflect upon them. That means parents can coach kids, help them build their brains, and develop mental health.

Drs. Siegel and Bryson offer a range of helpful insights for parents in their book.

First, connect and redirect. Often, kids get overwhelmed with feelings. Maybe they say something confusing like this: "Mom, you never leave me a note in the middle of the night and I hate homework!" When kids make unreasonable assertions, it's tempting to respond with demands:

> "That doesn't make any sense. And what are you doing out of bed? Go back to your room right now!"

This response addresses their left brain logic—but that's exactly what they're struggling to use! Instead of demands, connect with their right-brain emotions and redirect with left-brain logic:

> "Want me to leave you a note tonight? And I've got some ideas about homework, but it's late now, so let's talk more tomorrow."

This response shows them how they can accept their strong emotions and give them validity. But also sets a positive example of how they can bring their logic into play and make wise decisions.

Most of all, you're turning a moment of frustration into an opportunity to connect.

Second, name it to tame it. We usually want to simply move on when kids get overpowered with emotion. But this only coils up their deep feelings, causing them to spring back stronger later on. Instead, encourage kids to process their emotions out loud with you.

Siegel and Bryson share how one nine-year-old girl named Bella didn't want to flush the toilet after she saw it overflow once. To help her overcome her fear, her dad sat her down and asked her to tell the story. She recounted all the details—and soon her fears went away. Bella's dad helped her activate her left-brain logic. Their conversation let her walk through what happened and tame her anxieties with reason.

As a result, the two sides of her brain had the chance to practice working together.

Third, engage, don't enrage. When kids don't get what they want, their downstairs brain tends to take control, triggering a strong gut reaction. For example, let's say you didn't buy them a necklace that they wanted. They might lash out: "I hate you mommy!" Our natural instinct is to respond in kind with our own downstairs reaction:

"That is not ok to say. I don't want you to ever say that again!"

However, their downstairs brain can't thoughtfully process your correction. Instead, try engaging their upstairs brain:

Them: "I hate you!"
You: "Wow, you're really mad. Is it because I didn't get you that necklace?"
Them: "Yes! You're so mean!"
You: "That necklace wasn't for sale. It's ok if you want to keep feeling upset, but if you'd rather, we can be problem-solvers and think of another idea."

Fourth, use it or lose it. Kids need their downstairs and upstairs brains to flourish. But when they're little, their upstairs brain needs extra help.

If they rarely practice being thoughtful, they'll tend to rely too much on their gut and struggle to reach their full potential. As Siegel and Bryson put it:

> The upstairs brain is like a muscle: when it gets used, it develops, gets stronger, and performs better. And when it gets ignored, it doesn't develop optimally, losing some of its power and ability to function.

In other words, we need to let kids make decisions for themselves. They need the chance to weigh different options, consider alternatives, and think through the outcomes of their choices. That practice is critical for their brains to mature and grow stronger.

Fifth, move it or lose it. We tend to think our brains and bodies are two separate things. But they're actually intimately connected. As a result, physical activity can be a big help to kids when they're struggling to stay mentally balanced.

One mother shares how her son was struggling with his homework. When she entered his room, he was curled up into a ball under his bean bag. She encouraged him to sit down and try working again, but he couldn't make progress. Then, all of a sudden, he darted out of the house and ran several blocks. He came back, settled down, had a snack, and calmly finished his homework with his mom.

In short, a little exercise can go a long way when our kids (or we ourselves) are struggling.

In the above examples, the goal isn't to teach kids that some parts of their brains are bad and others are good. To live full lives, we need all four: emotions, instincts, logic, and thoughtfulness. The key is to help kids integrate the four parts so they can develop balanced, healthy brains.

With Siegel and Bryson's insights, we can gain a deeper understanding of our children. We can go from trying to survive the toughest moments with our kids to sparking deep conversations that'll help them thrive.

Never Split the Difference

Negotiation isn't only about business deals or hostage situations. Ultimately, it's the skill of *working with people*. That means everyone should learn negotiation—especially people who work with kids.

Working with kids is all about helping them learn to make good decisions. And that's what a good negotiator does too. They partner with people to help them think more clearly about their choices.

We tend to get negotiation wrong in two ways:

1. We think it's about making demands, or
2. We think it's about balanced compromises.

These misunderstandings lead to big problems.

First, making demands can lead kids to either rebel or give up. In other words, demands make kids feel like you're taking away their power. They'll either refuse and do their own thing, or disengage entirely.

Second, a balanced compromise isn't always the best outcome. Let's say a teenager wants to go clubbing all night on a Wednesday, but you compromise by letting them stay out late at a friend's house. That's balanced but not best. Teenagers need rest, especially on weeknights.

Great negotiators make people feel powerful and autonomous. They help people make the best possible choice by using their own critical thinking to analyze their decisions.

But how?!

Chris Voss talks about how to do this on The Knowledge Project podcast with Shane Parrish.[6] Chris is the former lead international kidnapping negotiator for the FBI and author of a must-read book entitled *Never Split the Difference*.[7] He found that his skills as a negotiator helped him with his kids as well.

Let's look at four of Chris's tactics.

First, use your voice strategically. Humans naturally copy the energy of the people they're around. As a result, you can shape the conversation by how you say what you say.

- Use a positive, playful voice most of the time. It'll help kids feel comfortable and encouraged.
- When they get anxious or upset, use the late-night FM DJ voice: slow, deep, and calm.
- Use an assertive voice sparingly, only for very important points, because it'll cause pushback.

Second, mirror their language. The best way to help someone think is to force them to reflect on what they're saying.

Don't critique their wrong ideas. Instead, repeat back to them the last few words from their last sentence.

Here's an example conversation:

Teenager: "I want to go to Club Sparkle with my friends."
You: "With your friends..."
Teenager: "Yeah, I've worked hard this semester and I think I earned a break."
You: "Earned a break..."
Teenager: "Well, they've asked me a few times and I've said no to study."
You: "No to study..."

Avoid sounding sassy or disapproving. The goal isn't to shame them or make them feel bad about their thought process. The goal is to keep them talking and open their eyes to their thinking. As a result, you'll help them analyze whether they're making good decisions on their own.

Third, label their emotions. People open up to new ideas when they feel understood. That's the power of empathy! We often get it wrong by making the conversation about us. We say things like: "Oh man, I know what that's like." We're trying to connect, but we actually make others feel unheard.

Don't say you know what they feel. Show it! Put a label on the emotions you see and then pause. Give them a chance to unpack and explain what they're feeling.

Here's an example:

Teenager: "Come on Dad, Club Sparkle would be so much fun."

You: "It sounds like you want to celebrate your hard work with your friends."

Teenager: "Yes! I've studied so much this year that I haven't been able to spend any time with my friends, and this is our last chance to hang out before graduation."

Labels will give you a chance to verify what you think they're feeling. They make others feel like you're listening and seriously considering their emotions. They also help them develop more self-awareness of their own perspective.

Fourth, ask open questions. The last tactic is to ask genuine questions that get kids thinking. For example, instead of saying "No" to Club Sparkle, you could ask: "How am I supposed to let you stay out so late at a club?" Start with "how" and make sure it's an open-ended question, not yes or no.

Your goal is to engage them and draw them into the problem-solving process. You're challenging them to take responsibility to find a better alternative for themselves.

These strategies will help you build a strong relationship as you work through hard problems together. They are more effective for creating solutions that are best for everyone. You're also setting an example for how your kids can work well with other people themselves.

I hope you find all of the above ideas and tactics helpful. For more insights, check out the books themselves. They're filled with engaging stories, practical tips, and thoughtful reflections on how we can work with kids (and adults) more effectively.

Afterword
by Chrisman Frank

I T ALL STARTED, as so many things do these days, with a tweet:

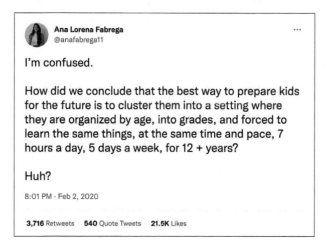

I hadn't heard of Ana yet (she only had 100 or so followers at the time). But I immediately knew she would become a force to be reckoned with in the world of education.

At the time, I was kicking around the idea of starting an education company with my friend Josh Dahn, another world-class teacher who cofounded Ad Astra School with Elon Musk. So, I reached out to Ana to get her opinion.

We connected over video chat. She was charismatic and articulate (despite English being her third language). Everyone has opinions about education, but Ana spoke with the authority of an experienced practitioner and the curiosity of a novice.

When Josh and I decided to pull the trigger and start Synthesis, Ana had (as predicted) taken Twitter by storm as THE go-to source for novel insights about education. She joined the very first Synthesis session as an observer, wrote our launch post to her 20k+ followers, and joined as our Chief Evangelist a few months later.

Our expectations for her were simple: just keep being Ana. Keep being a voracious learning machine. Keep talking to hundreds of kids and parents. And most of all, keep sharing insights with the world.

The more people Ana reaches with her message, we realized, the better shot we have at solving humanity's most critical problems.

Why?

Because Ana presents a fresh perspective on the issue that, today, the system that educates our children is broken; an issue we believe to be of civilizational importance.

Our system has failed to leverage the unprecedented tools we have—computers, mainly—to ensure we raise the next billion humans as determined problem-solvers. Traditional schooling was built for a prior era: one of assembly lines and mass indoctrination. And it hasn't kept up. It's embarrassing that, in 2023, we still require kids to color inside the lines and follow instructions without question.

Human capital is our scarcest resource and the bottleneck to civilizational progress. Course-correcting how we educate humanity's future generations must be our top priority. And while not everyone acknowledges this today, I'm ecstatic that a voice like Ana is emerging to spread the message.

Her first book represents a small dose of optimism amid our obsolete educational structures. I read it with a smile. We have work to do, I keep telling myself, but I'm confident we are headed in the right direction.

I hope you enjoyed reading *The Learning Game* as much as I did.

Acknowledgments

I have so many people to thank for their contributions to this book. My parents, for instilling in me a love for learning. The Harriman House team, for taking a chance on me and making it all come true. David Perell, for inspiring me to write and supporting my work. Chrisman Frank, for believing in me and encouraging me all along the way. Janis Ozolins, for the spot-on illustrations. James Baird, for overseeing the publishing process. Sylvia Scodro and Polina Pompliano, for their invaluable contributions and feedback. And, most of all, my husband Fernando, whose shining intellect and editing has elevated my work, and whose faith gives me hope that I might one day become the person he is convinced I have always been.

Endnotes

Chapter 1

1 John Taylor Gatto, "I Quit, I Think," *The Wall Street Journal* (July 25, 1991).

2 John Taylor Gatto, *Dumbing Us Down* (Vancouver: New Society Publishers, 1992).

3 Gatto, *Dumbing Us Down*, 1.

4 Gatto, *Dumbing Us Down*, 3-4.

5 Gatto, *Dumbing Us Down*, 5.

6 "Multitasking: Switching Costs," American Psychological Association (March 20, 2006).

7 Gatto, *Dumbing Us Down*, 6.

8 Gatto, *Dumbing Us Down*, 7.

9 Gatto, *Dumbing Us Down*, 8-9.

10 Gatto, *Dumbing Us Down*, 9.

Chapter 2

1 James Van Horn Melton, *Absolutism and the Eighteenth-Century Origins of Compulsory Schooling in Prussia and Austria* (New York: Cambridge University Press, 2003).

2 Johann Gottlieb Fichte, *Addresses to the German Nation* (Chicago: The Open Court Publishing Company, 1922), 21.

3 Ellwood Patterson Cubberley, *The History of Education: Educational Practice and Progress Considered as a Phase of the Development and Spread of Western Civilization* (New York: Houghton Mifflin, 1920).

4 Max Roser and Esteban Ortiz-Ospina, "Literacy," Our World in Data (September 20, 2018).

5   Arthur Herman, *Freedom's Forge: How American Business Produced Victory in World War II* (New York: Random House, 2012).

6   This trend originated in the early 20th century, but flowered into full bloom after World War II. See John Taylor Gatto, *The Underground History of American Education* (2000), 204-230.

7   Sharon L. Nichols and David C. Berliner, *Collateral Damage: How High-Stakes Testing Corrupts America's Schools* (Cambridge, MA: Harvard Education Press, 2007).

8   "NAEP Long-Term Trend Assessment Results: Reading and Mathematics," National Center for Education Statistics, 2022.

9   Robert Gordon, *The Rise and Fall of American Growth* (Princeton: Princeton University Press, 2016); Tyler Cowen, *The Great Stagnation* (New York: Dutton, 2011).

10 Jonathan Rothwell, "Assessing the Economic Gains of Eradicating Illiteracy Nationally and Regionally in the United States," Barbara Bush Foundation for Family Literacy (September 8, 2020).

11 Jeffrey M. Jones, "Confidence in U.S. Institutions Down; Average at New Low," gallup.com (July 5, 2022).

12 For more on Lego's business strategy, see Jan W. Rivkin, Stefan Thomke, and Daniela Beyersdorfer, "Lego," Harvard Business School Case 613-004 (July 2012).

13 "Lego: Latest Usage and Revenue Statistics," lightailing.com (May 16, 2022).

14 Page Moreau and Marit Gundersen Engeset, "The Downstream Consequences of Problem-Solving Mindsets: How Playing with Lego Influences Creativity," *Journal of Marketing Research* 53, no 1 (2016): 18-30.

15 Derek Cabrera, "How Thinking Works," TEDxWilliamsport, youtube.com (December 6, 2011).

16 Seth Godin, "Stop Stealing Dreams," TEDxYouth, youtube.com (October 16, 2012).

Chapter 3

1   Alan Blinder, "Atlanta Educators Convicted in School Cheating Scandal," *The New York Times* (April 1, 2015).

2   For a modern example of the research, see Nathan Kuncel and Sarah Hezlett, "Standardized Tests Predict Graduate Students' Success," *Science* 315, no. 5815 (February 23, 2007): 1080-1081.

3   See Sharon L. Nichols and David C. Berliner, *Collateral Damage: How High-Stakes Testing Corrupts America's Schools* (Boston: Harvard Education Press, 2007), chapter 1.

4   See Nichols and Berliner, *Collateral Damage*, chapter 7.

5   Nathaniel von der Embse, Dane Jester, Devlina Roy, and James Post, "Test Anxiety Effects, Predictors, and Correlates: A 30-Year Meta-Analytic Review," *Journal of Affective Disorders* 227 (2018): 483–493.

6   See Nichols and Berliner, *Collateral Damage*, chapters 2–3.

7   Zubair Ahmed Khan to parents of students at International Indian School – Dammam (January 15, 2020).

8   Daniel Pink, "The Puzzle of Motivation," TED Talk, ted.com (July 2009).

9   Polina Pompliano, "The Profile Dossier: Esther Wojcicki, the Educator Who Raised Entrepreneurial Children," theprofile.substack.com (May 19, 2021).

Chapter 4

1   Alvin Toffler, *Future Shock* (New York: Bantam, 1984), 414.

2   Anne-Laure Le Cunff, "The Forgetting Curve: The Science of How Fast We Forget," nesslabs.com (n.d.).

Chapter 6

1   Paul Graham, "A Project of One's Own," paulgraham.com (June 2021).

2   Ibid.

3   Julie Sygiel, "How The Visionary Founder Behind Jeni's Splendid Churned Her Ice Cream Dreams Into Reality," *Forbes* (February 28, 2018).

4   Paul Graham, "How to Think for Yourself," paulgraham.com (November 2020).

5   Adam Grant, *Originals* (New York: Penguin, 2017), 4.

6   Ibid., 1–2.

7   Ibid.

8   Jordan Crook, "Warby Parker, Valued at $3 Billion, Raises $245 Million in Funding," techcrunch.com (August 27, 2020).

9   Warren Berger, *A More Beautiful Question* (London: Bloomsbury, 2014), 83.

10 Grant, *Originals*, 7.

11 Robert Sutton, *Weird Ideas That Work* (New York: Free Press, 2007), 25.

Chapter 7

1   See Jean Clottes, *What Is Paleolithic Art?* (Chicago: University of Chicago, 2016).

2   Personal correspondence.

3   Shane Parrish, "Predicting the Future with Bayes' Theorem," fs.blog (n.d.).

Chapter 8

1   Joshua Foer, *Moonwalking with Einstein* (New York: Penguin, 2011).

2   Ibid.

Chapter 9

1   Shaylene Nancekivell, Priti Shah, and Susan Gelman, "Maybe They're Born With It, or Maybe It's Experience: Toward a Deeper Understanding of the Learning Style Myth," *Journal of Educational Psychology* 112, no. 2 (Feburary 2020): 221-235.

2   VARK stands for visual, aural, read/write, and kinesthetic. Learn more at vark-learn.com.

3   See Nancekivell, Shah, and Gelman, "Maybe They're Born With It, or Maybe It's Experience."

4   See, e.g., James Clark and Allan Paivio, "Dual Coding Theory and Education," *Educational Psychology Review* 3, no. 3 (1991): 149-210; Frank Coffield, David Moseley, Elaine Hall, and Kathryn Ecclestone, *Learning Styles and Pedagogy in Post-16 Learning* (London: Learning and Skills Research Center, 2004).

5   Polly Husmann and Valerie Dean O'Loughlin, "Another Nail in the Coffin for Learning Styles?" *Anatomical Science Education* 12, no. 1 (2018): 6-19.

6   Carol Dweck, *Mindset* (New York: Ballantine, 2007).

Chapter 10

1   Sidney D'Mello and Art Graesser, "Dynamics of Affective States during Complex Learning," *Learning and Instruction* 22, no. 2 (April 2012): 145-157.

2   As quoted in "Confusion Can Be Beneficial for Learning," University of Notre Dame, ScienceDaily (June 20, 2012).

3   Barry Wadsworth, *Piaget's Theory of Cognitive and Affective Development* (5th ed.; London: Pearson, 2003).

4 Peter Holley, "Elon Musk Created a Secretive 'Laboratory School' for Brilliant Kids Who Love Flamethrowers," Washington Post (June 27, 2018).

Chapter 11

1 As quoted in George Kalmpourtzis, *Educational Game Design Fundamentals* (London: Taylor & Francis, 2018), 68.

2 Jane McGonigal, "How Games Make Life Better," Invest Like the Best podcast (July 2019).

3 Jane McGonigal, *Reality Is Broken* (New York: Penguin, 2011), 25.

4 Clay Risen, "Mihaly Csikszentmihalyi, the Father of 'Flow,' Dies at 87," *The New York Times* (October 28, 2021).

5 Suzanne Prescott and Mihály Csíkszentmihályi, "Environmental Effects on Cognitive and Affective States: The Experiential Time Sampling Approach," Social Behavior and Personality 9, no. 1 (1981): 23-32.

6 For more on flow, see Mihály Csíkszentmihályi, *Flow* (New York: HarperCollins, 2008).

7 See ibid., chapter 4.

8 James Vincent, "Amazon Turns Warehouse Tasks into Video Games to Make Work 'Fun,'" The Verge (May 22, 2019).

9 See Margaret Robertson, "Can't Play, Won't Play," Kotaku (November 10, 2010); and Elisa Mekler, "Do Points, Levels and Leaderboards Harm Intrinsic Motivation?" University of Waterloo Stratford School, youtube.com (January 29, 2014).

10 McGonigal, "How Games Make Life Better."

11 Ibid.

12 Ibid.

13 Ibid.

14 For more on flow, see Csíkszentmihályi, *Flow*.

15 Mark Rober, "Tricking Your Brain into Learning More," TEDxPenn, youtube.com (May 31, 2018).

16 Ibid.

17 Alison Millington, "J. K. Rowling's pitch for 'Harry Potter' was rejected 12 times—read the now-famous letter here," *Insider* (July 31, 2018).

18 Madison Malone-Kircher, "James Dyson on 5,126 Vacuums That Didn't Work—and the One That Finally Did," *New York Magazine* (November 22, 2016).

19 Katie Gilsenan, "The Next Gen: Getting to Know Kids' Relationship with Video Games," gwi.com (July 27, 2021).

Chapter 12

1 "Generation M2: Media in the Lives of 8- to 18-Year-Olds," Kaiser Family Foundation (January 2010).

2 Richard Ryan and Edward Deci, "Self-Determination Theory and the Facilitation of Intrinsic Motivation, Social Development, and Well-Being," *American Psychologist* 55, no. 1 (2000): 68–78.

3 Nir Eyal, "Kids' Gaming Obsession Isn't Really About the Games," *Psychology Today* (August 19, 2018). See also Nir Eyal, *Indistractable* (Dallas, Texas: BenBella, 2019).

4 Robert Epstein, "The Myth of the Teen Brain," *Scientific American* (June 1, 2007).

5 Eyal, *Indistractable*, 197.

6 See, for example, Craig Anderson and Karen Dill, "Video Games and Aggressive Thoughts, Feelings, and Behavior in the Laboratory and in Life," *Journal of Personality and Social Psychology* 78, no. 4 (2000): 772–790.

7 Jane McGonigal, *SuperBetter* (New York: Penguin, 2016), 415–424.

Chapter 13

1 Nassim Taleb, *Skin in the Game* (New York: Random House, 2018).

2 Ibid., 30.

3 See Josh's Twitter thread on his journey toward designing the Synthesis simulations, published on September 7, 2021: https://twitter.com/josh_dahn/status/1435240843389046784

Chapter 14

1 See Greg Lukianoff and Jonathan Heidt, *The Coddling of the American Mind* (Penguin Press, 2018).

2 Nassim Taleb, *Antifragile* (New York: Random House, 2012).

Chapter 16

1 See David Epstein, *Range* (New York: Penguin, 2019), introduction.

2 See Ashley Fetters, "The Case Against Grit," *The Atlantic* (May 31, 2019).

3 Epstein, *Range*, 33.

4 Ibid., 198.

5   Eric Jorgenson, *The Almanack of Naval Ravikant* (n.p.: Magrathea Publishing, 2020), 41.

6   Ibid.

Chapter 17

1   John Holt, *How Children Fail* (Lebanon, IN: Da Capo Lifelong, 1995).

2   Stuart Firestein, *Failure* (New York: Oxford University Press, 2015).

3   See Naval's tweet published on Janurary 23, 2020: https://twitter.com/naval/status/1220309894210846722

4   Firestein, *Failure*, 1.

5   See Martin Seligman, *Learned Optimism* (New York: Vintage, 2011).

6   See Martin Seligman, *The Optimistic Child* (New York: HarperOne, 2007).

7   Deepak Malhotra, "Tragedy & Genius," Speech to Graduating MBA Students, Harvard Business School, April 23, 2012.

8   Ibid.

9   It appears as if Kristin Levitan has since removed the blog post where she made this statement.

10 Michelle Obama, *Becoming* (New York: Penguin, 2018), xv.

11 "Futurework: Trends and Challenges for Work in the 21st Century," U.S. Department of Labor, September 1, 1999.

12 "Number of Jobs, Labor Market Experience, Marital Status, and Health: Results from a National Longitudinal Survey," Bureau of Labor Statistics, August 31, 2021.

13 Adam Grant, *Think Again* (New York: Penguin, 2021), 231.

14 Ibid., 232.

Chapter 18

1   Charles Duhigg, *Smarter Faster Better* (New York: Random House, 2016), 86-88.

2   As quoted in ibid., 86.

3   James Clear, "Mental Models: Learn How to Think Better and Gain a Mental Edge," jamesclear.com (n.d.).

4   Ibid.

5   Charlie Munger, "A Lesson on Elementary, Worldly Wisdom as It Relates to Investment Management and Business," USC Business School (May 5, 1994).

6   Ibid.

7   Abraham Maslow, *The Psychology of Science* (New York: HarperCollins, 1966).

8   Jonah Berger, *The Catalyst* (New York: Simon & Schuster, 2020).

9   Richard Thaler and Cass Sunstein, *Nudge: The Final Edition* (New York: Penguin, 2021).

10 Thomas Wedell-Wedellsborg, *What Your Problem?* (Boston: Harvard Business Review, 2020).

11 Andrew Wilkinson, "The Power of Anti-Goals," medium.com (July 6, 2017)..

12 See fs.blog

13 Gabriel Weinberg and Lauren McCann, *Super Thinking* (New York: Penguin, 2019).

14 See Atul Gawande, *The Checklist Manifesto* (New York: Metropolitan, 2009).

Chapter 19

1   Edward De Bono, *Teach Your Child How to Think* (New York: Penguin, 2017).

2   Ibid.

3   See Philip Tetlock and Dan Gardner, *Superforecasting* (New York: Penguin, 2015).

4   Annie Duke, *Thinking Bets* (New York: Penguin, 2018).

5   Ibid., 7–10.

6   Ibid., 5–7.

7   Tetlock and Gardner, *Superforecasting*.

8   Leonard Mlodinow, *Elastic* (New York: Penguin, 2018).

9   See Robert Chialdini, *Influence* (New York: HarperCollins, 1984).

10 Mark Robert Anderson, "Twenty Years on from Deep Blue vs Kasparov: How a Chess Match Started the Big Data Revolution," *The Conversation* (n.d.).

11 Mlodinow, *Elastic*, 7–10.

How to Exit the System

1   Taleb, *Antifragile*, 316–320.

2   See galileoxp.com

3   See forestschoolassociation.org

4   See synthesis.com

5   See arduino.cc

6   See brilliant.org, skillshare.com, and khanacademy.org

7   See montessori.org, waldorfeducation.org, and reggioalliance.org

8   See soraschools.com, tohigherground.com, and actonacademy.org

9   See prenda.com

Ms. Fab Book Recommendations

1   Esther Wojcicki, *How To Raise Successful People* (New York: HarperCollins, 2019).

2   Ibid., 61–62.

3   Ibid., 120.

4   Ibid., 158.

5   Daniel Siegel and Tina Payne Bryson, *The Whole-Brain Child* (New York: Penguin, 2011).

6   Chris Voss, "The Art of Letting Other People Have Your Way," The Knowledge Project podcast (October 2019).

7   Chris Voss with Tahl Raz, *Never Split the Difference* (New York: HarperCollins, 2016).

Index